THE GROWTH

OF

PLATO'S IDEAL THEORY

The Growth of Plato's Ideal theory.

I, ct.

The earliest Greek philosophies were philosophies of Being. The end which the thinkers of these days proposed to themselves was the discovery of the ultimate reality of the physical universe; in other words they occupied themselves with the object of Knowledge to the exclusion of the Knowing subject. But it is impossible for man to investigate Being in itself; he can regard reality only as it is reflected in his own mind, he can reach Being only through Knowing. the "cogito" comes first, the "sum", "est" "sunt" &c. are only inferences from it. Then only can we proceed to speak of the reality of objects when we have shown that the mind is a faithful, not a distorted mirror. all this the Pre-Socratic philosophy as a whole overlooked. And it was natural that it should. The child looks outward; reflection, the turning of the mind inward on itself, comes only in later life. The days of the Ionic, Eleatic, & Pythagorean schools were the childhood of philosophy; reflection began with Socrates. The philosophy of Socrates, Plato, & Aristotle as distinguished from the early theories of Being, was essentially a philosophy of Knowing; it turned the side of the medal which had been neglected by previous thinkers, the subject; and its theories of the object or of Being were deductions from its theories of Knowing. In a word, previous philosophies had been objective, the new philosophy was subjective.

FIRST PAGE OF MS. OF "THE GROWTH OF
PLATO'S IDEAL THEORY" (¾ nat. size)

THE GROWTH OF
PLATO'S IDEAL THEORY
AN ESSAY

BY

SIR JAMES GEORGE FRAZER

O.M., F.R.S., F.B.A.

FELLOW OF TRINITY COLLEGE, CAMBRIDGE
MEMBRE DE L'INSTITUT DE FRANCE

NEW YORK / RUSSELL & RUSSELL

FIRST PUBLISHED BY MACMILLAN & CO., LONDON

REISSUED, 1967, BY RUSSELL & RUSSELL

A DIVISION OF ATHENEUM HOUSE, INC.

BY ARRANGEMENT WITH TRINITY COLLEGE, CAMBRIDGE UNIVERSITY

L. C. CATALOG CARD NO: 66−27072

PRINTED IN ·THE UNITED STATES OF AMERICA

PREFACE

SOME apology is perhaps due to my readers for presenting to them an essay which was written more than fifty years ago, and which I have not attempted to bring into line with the subsequent growth of Platonic studies. In explanation or excuse I would say that Plato is an old love of mine, and that I had read the whole of his works in the original before I took my first degree at Cambridge in 1878. Accordingly, when in competing for a Fellowship at Trinity College in 1879 I had to write a dissertation to be submitted to the examiners, I naturally chose for my subject the theory which more than any other is associated with the name of Plato. Since then I have neglected Platonic studies for others far remote from them, but reviewing my youthful essay after the lapse of half a century I am encouraged to believe that it truly represents the rise and fall of the Ideal Theory in Plato's mind ; hence I venture to publish it exactly as I wrote it, without any attempt, apart from a few minute corrections, either to improve the matter or to polish the style. Only, in order to smooth the path for the reader, I have relegated most of the references and Greek quotations to the notes at the foot of the page.

The question of the growth of Plato's Ideal Theory is intimately bound up with the question of the chronological order of the Platonic dialogues, and if I were to rewrite my essay I should probably express a different view as to the dates of some of the dialogues, particularly the *Phaedrus* and the *Theaetetus*, both of which I now believe to be posterior to the *Republic*. But any such changes in the dating would not materially affect my conclusions, which are based directly on Plato's own words and on nothing else. The earlier dates which, with some hesitation, I have assigned to the *Phaedrus* and *Theaetetus* in my essay, were adopted to a certain extent in deference to the opinion of my revered teacher and friend, Henry Jackson, whose lectures on Plato I regularly attended at Trinity. But both these dialogues bear clear traces of a late date in their literary style, for the complicated and cumbrous construction of the sentences in them contrasts sharply with the easy and natural flow of the sentences in the earlier dialogues, which are perfect models of pellucid Attic prose at its best, like the histories of Xenophon and the speeches of Lysias, with none of that obvious straining after an artificial smoothness which mars the otherwise elegant prose of Plato's literary rival, Isocrates. And with the marked change for the worse in the construction of the sentences there goes a still deeper change in the whole cast and setting of the pieces; for in the later dialogues, always with the exception of the *Phaedrus*, the dramatic element has really disappeared, though the form of a dialogue is preserved. The vivacious manner of a great dramatist, enthralling his hearers by the alternate play of high tragedy and light comedy, is exchanged for the dryasdust manner of a professor lecturing to docile pupils, who have little more to do than to assent passively to the doctrines inculcated on them by their master. It is a transformation like that of a Shakespeare into a Kant.

Since my essay was written the change in Plato's literary style has been carefully investigated by a number of scholars, notably by the Polish scholar Wincenty Lutoslawski, and the German scholar Constantin Ritter, who have used the linguistic evidence as an important and often decisive test to determine the chronological sequence of the dialogues. With their conclusions I am in general agreement, particularly in regard to the dating of the dialogues which followed the *Republic*, all of which, with the possible exception of the *Parmenides*, are written in Plato's later and far inferior manner. By a coincidence, which can hardly be accidental, the change in the writer's style appears to have been nearly, though not quite, contemporary with his final renunciation of the Ideal Theory. It is as if, with the fading of the Ideas from his heaven, the world had lost its brightness for the philosopher, and henceforth he walked in darkness, or at most in a grey twilight, guided by the pale cold light of Reason instead of by the purple glow of Imagination. It is true that in the *Phaedrus* the Ideas blaze up in all their splendour, but it was for the last time; it was the sunset glory, the rosy flush on the clouds that hung about the descending luminary. They had come like clouds in the meridian of Plato's fancy, and like clouds they vanished in the evening of his days. In the deepening shadows the dreamer awoke, and behold it was a dream.

J. G. FRAZER

January 1930

THE ARGUMENT

I. The earliest Greek philosophies of Being—The philosophy of Socrates a theory of Knowing—His method introspective—The process of generalization—The pyramid of knowledge—The method of Induction the instrument of modern science—Barrenness of the Socratic Induction—Discouragement of pure science—Generalization a mark at once of the strength and the weakness of the human mind—The imperfection of general notions.

II. Plato's splendid error—The conversion of a true theory of knowledge into a false theory of being—Two groups of Plato's writings, the Socratic dialogues and the Platonic—The Socratic dialogues—The *Euthyphro, Laches, Hippias Major, Charmides*—Characteristics of the Socratic dialogues—Anticipations of later views—Hints of Platonic Ideas.

III. The Ideal Theory the great feature of the second group of Platonic dialogues—The *Theaetetus* a mature work of Plato—A search after knowledge through sensation—The date of the *Theaetetus*—The style of the *Theaetetus*—Is knowledge sensation ? The limits of sensation—The combination of sensations—The notions of things—Things but groups of sensations—Notions of pure reason—Theory of sensation—Sensation a product of motion—The flux of sensation—Negative conclusion of the *Theaetetus*.

IV. The *Cratylus*, a search after knowledge through words—The relation of words to things—Admission of an absolute existence—Words the copies of things—Element of convention in words—Knowledge not to be had by words—First appearance of the Platonic Ideas—Ideas the elements of things.

V. The *Meno*—The Ideal Theory used to prove the immortality of the soul by means of reminiscence—The *Meno, Phaedrus*, and *Symposium*—The doctrine of immortality—Knowledge before birth—The doctrine of reminiscence.

VI. The *Phaedrus*—The Ideal Theory in the *Phaedrus*—The Idea of

THE GROWTH

OF

PLATO'S IDEAL THEORY

I

THE earliest Greek philosophies were philosophies of Being. The end which the thinkers of these days proposed to themselves was the discovery of the ultimate reality of the physical universe ; in other words, they occupied themselves with the object of Knowledge to the exclusion of the Knowing subject. But it is impossible for man to investigate Being in itself ; he can regard reality only as it is reflected in his own mind, he can reach Being only through Knowing ; the " *cogito* " comes first, the " *sum* ", " *est* ", " *sunt* ", etc., are only inferences from it. Then only can we proceed to speak of the reality of objects when we have shown that the mind is a faithful, not a distorted mirror. All this the Pre-Socratic philosophy as a whole overlooked. And it was natural that it should. The child looks outward ; reflection, the turning of the mind inward on itself, comes only in later life. The days of the Ionic, Eleatic, and Pythagorean schools were the childhood of philosophy ; reflection began with Socrates. The philosophy of Socrates, Plato, and Aristotle as distinguished from the early theories of Being was essentially a philosophy of Knowing ; it turned the side of the medal which had been neglected by previous thinkers, the subject ; and its theories of the object or of Being were deductions from its theories of Knowing. In a word previous philosophies had been objective, the new philosophy was subjective. This movement begun by Socrates was necessary : if men were ever to know the outward world it was needful that they should first obey the oracle by knowing themselves. Socrates, who inaugurated this great movement, hardly got beyond a theory of Knowing ; but his theory of knowledge was the foundation on which Plato and Aristotle reared their vast theories of Being.

Before Socrates philosophers had built up different theories of the universe, but had failed to examine the foundation on which all such theories must rest—the mind. Wanting this foundation, these early theories were incapable of proof. Even when these philosophers turned their attention to the mind, they [1] viewed it simply as a part of the physical universe. Socrates turned away from the external to examine the internal world, from nature he turned to man.[2] To inquire into the former before we have made ourselves acquainted with the latter was, to his mind, folly.[3] Hence the famous saying of Cicero that Socrates brought down philosophy from heaven to earth, and gave it a dwelling in the cities and homes of men.[4] But for philosophy this dwelling is after all too narrow ; for while there is a philosophy which limits us to the immediate and the present, there is another which leads us or seems to lead us from the immediate and the present to the distant in space and time, away once more to that sky from which Socrates called it down to earth.

But Socrates differed from his predecessors not only in the object but in the method of his inquiry. For a physical he substituted a psychological or introspective method ; instead of explaining the mind by physical causes, he watched its internal workings without any reference to its ultimate composition or substance. While his method was thus an inward one (if I may use the expression), it was still not inward enough, it was not purely psychological, it was much more logical. He looked to the processes or workings of our intellectual faculties and the results they gave, without inquiring into the faculties themselves and the nature of the mind in general ; he investigated the acts, not the powers. Even of these acts or processes his investigation was but superficial, nor did his great pupil Plato supply the defect ; it was left for Aristotle to reduce the mental operations by which we pass from the known to the unknown,

---

[1] E.g. Heraclitus ap. Ritt. and Prell. §§ 32, 33 ; Empedocles, ib. § 139.
[2] Xen. Mem. i. 1. 11-16 ; Plato, Phaedr. p. 229 E sqq.
[3] ἐσκόπει πότερά ποτε νομίσαντες

ἱκανῶς ἤδη τἀνθρώπινα εἰδέναι ἔρχονται ἐπὶ τὸ περὶ τῶν τοιούτων φροντίζειν, ἢ τὰ μὲν ἀνθρώπεια παρέντες τὰ δαιμόνια δὲ σκοποῦντες ἡγοῦνται τὰ προσήκοντα πράττειν. Xen. Mem. l.c. § 12.
[4] Cic. Tusc. Disp. v. 4.

in short our inferences, to two great classes, induction and deduction. Thus it was not the operations of mind in general which Socrates investigated, it was only the process of inference or reasoning ; the mental powers which are sub-servient to these processes (such as sensation, memory, imagination) he apparently took for granted without in-vestigation. It was the method of reasoning, inference, or classification on which he bestowed thought, and undoubtedly he grasped this process in its general outline correctly enough. This process is in brief generalization. Only through the power of generalization have we any knowledge that is of practical value. But for this power and the processes immediately subordinate to it, I mean memory, abstraction, comparison, our mental life would be but a train of fleeting sensations, between which we would be aware of no connexion. The same sensation might occur thousands of times, but, without the powers I have mentioned, it would on every occasion present itself as a fresh sensation, our past existence would be unknown, our future unthought of, we would have nothing but the present sensation. From this dismal state we are rescued first by the powers of memory and compari-son. When the sensation is gone, an image of it is stored up in the mind, and when the same (*i.e.* an exactly similar) sensation is repeated, the image of the former similar sensation is called up and compared with the present sensation, and thus the identity of the two is recognized through the medium of the image preserved in memory. This power of memory, while it raises the mind above the state of pure sensation, would in itself be of little use, seeing that it would only enable us to recognize those sensations which were identical with (exactly similar to) others which we had experienced before. It would enable us, *e.g.*, to recognize a particular table or stick which we had seen before, if the table or stick were presented to us in circumstances (those of light, position, distance, etc.) identical with those in which either had been presented before, but a change in one of the circumstances, *e.g.* in the light, would be enough to prevent the recognition. Our memory would consist of impressions or marks received from sensations, but into these impressions nothing could fit save the original die. Thus it is doubtful whether we could recognize even our parents or most intimate friends, since the sensations with which they affect us are hardly ever exactly similar. Out of this state again we are rescued by the powers of abstraction and generalization, which enable us to fix our attention upon points in which certain objects resemble each other, to the exclusion of those in which they differ. Thus we apprehend what we call the same and similar objects.

The difference between sameness and similarity (or rather between our knowledge of the one and our knowledge of the other) is really one of degree : when an object is presented to us, which in the vast majority of its qualities resembles one of which we have had previous experience, we say it is the same object ; when, along with certain resemblances, the object possesses a certain proportion of differences, we say the object is similar, and its similarity varies as this proportion of differences is less or greater. It is not likely that a man ever sees his father twice alike, yet the impressions received at different times from the object he calls his father resemble each other so much more than they differ from each other, that the man has no hesitation in saying that the object which gives rise to the various impressions is the same, that it is in all cases his father. Thus it is clear that in order to apprehend even what we call the same object, the power of generalization must be exercised. We have to compare a number of previous impressions, abstract from them the points in which they resemble each other to the exclusion of the points in which they differ, and unite these points of resemblance into one notion, which notion we identify with the image of the object presented by sense. Thus the recognition, *e.g.* of our father or mother, of King's Chapel, or the fountain in the great court of Trinity, is really the result of a rapid generalization. And if this is so, we must evidently concede to some of the lower animals what has been long denied them, the power of generalization. Only this power can enable a dog to recognize his master at different times and in different circumstances, when that master is standing up or lying down, in a blue coat or in a grey, with an angry or pleased expression of countenance. Generalization is more obviously, if not more really, exercised in the recognition of what we call similar objects. The only difference between what we call the same and similar objects consists, as I have said, in the number of the resemblances between the impressions which the objects have made on us. When that number is very great, we say that the object which gives rise to those similar impressions is the same ; when the number is not so great, we say that the objects are similar. But in the fact that similar objects are (perhaps in all languages) sometimes described as the same, we may see an indication of a consciousness that after all the difference between the two is one of degree, not of kind. When Heine (to take a lovely instance) says

> Die Kleine gleicht der Geliebten,
> Besonders wenn sie lacht ;
> Sie hat dieselben Augen,
> Die mich so elend gemacht,

no one would think of a Gorgon-like community of eyes between the little one and the beloved, even if the poet had not indicated by the first of these lines that by sameness he really meant similarity.

A higher power of generalization is required to discern similar than to discern the same ; for the fewer the points of resemblance, the higher the power required to detect them. It is hardly necessary to observe that the lower animals possess this power in a sufficiently high degree to enable them to recognize similar objects. A dog recognizes a dog as a dog, though he may never have seen the identical animal before. Thus the power of generalization (resting on memory, comparison, and abstraction) reduces what would be otherwise an unconnected train of sensations to an orderly system of knowledge ; objects are referred to classes, these classes to higher classes, and so on. Our knowledge is a pyramid, of which particulars are the base, and the highest generalization the pinnacle.

The discovery of this law of our thinking was due to Socrates. His discourses, as preserved to us by Xenophon and illustrated by the earlier, rightly called Socratic, dialogues of Plato, chiefly exemplify, though they do not analyse, the process of generalization.[1] And while Xenophon and Plato afford us examples of his discourses, Aristotle distinctly informs us of the principle on which they were based. In his sketch of the history of philosophy he tells us that Socrates, neglecting cosmology, sought to discover universals in moral questions, and gave his attention to definitions.[2] Again in the *Metaphysics* [3] he says that while definitions of physical things had been attempted to a small extent by previous philosophers as Democritus and the Pythagoreans, Socrates was the first who in the sphere of ethics sought for universal definitions: but previous attempts at definition had been very imperfect;[4] he assigns to Socrates as his speciality induction and definition.[5]

This then was the valuable discovery of Socrates, that all practically useful knowledge of individual things is only attainable through general notions, and so far as it went, this doctrine was true and useful. It was simply a doctrine of knowing, not of being. When Socrates asked (Xenophon *l.c.*) what is the beautiful, the ugly, and so on, he did not mean to ask after the particular mode of existence to which the term Beauty might be applied; all he wished to know was, what is our conception of beauty? "What is Beauty?" meant for him, what is our notion of beauty? The same question, what is beauty? meant for his pupil Plato something very different and received a very different answer. The Socratic theory of knowing was turned into the Platonic (and Aristotelian) theory of being.

But before going on to consider this great error, there are some observations which suggest themselves on the Socratic doctrine of knowledge. Though correct, it was barren, because it sought notions (*Begriffe*) not truths. Now a notion is single, a truth is double, it is the union of two notions as subject and predicate ; and as in nature, so in thought,

---

[1] Cf. Xenophon, *Mem.* i. 1. 16 αὐτὸς δὲ περὶ τῶν ἀνθρωπείων ἂν ἀεὶ διελέγετο, σκοπῶν τί εὐσεβές, τί ἀσεβές· τί καλόν, τί αἰσχρόν· τί δίκαιον, τί ἄδικον· τί σωφροσύνη, τί μανία· τί ἀνδρεία, τί δειλία· τί πόλις, τί πολιτικός· τί ἀρχὴ ἀνθρώπων, τί ἀρχικὸς ἀνθρώπων. Cf. Xen. *Mem.* iv. 5; 12 ;

[2] *Met.* 987 b 1-4.

[3] *Met.* iv. p. 1078 b 17 *sqq.*

[4] διαλεκτικὴ γὰρ ἰσχὺς οὔπω τότ' ἦν.

[5] δύο γάρ ἐστιν ἅ τις ἂν ἀποδοίη Σωκράτει δικαίως, τούς τ' ἐπακτικοὺς λόγους καὶ τὸ ὁρίζεσθαι καθόλου. Cp. *Part. An.* A c. 1, p. 642 a 24 *sqq.*

ib. 6; 1 ; *ib.* 13.

the solitary is barren, production is only made possible by union. Induction in the hands of Socrates was used as an instrument to the formation of notions or conceptions ; but these notions remained barren, being alone. With us Induction is used as an instrument to the attainment of truths, of true propositions, and the result is the vast discoveries of modern science. Do what he could, it was impossible for Socrates to reach anything fresh by his method, for we get out of a notion only what we choose to put into it. To expect to get more would be as idle as to expect to get more energy out at one end of a machine than we put in at the other. For a general notion is simply a mental collection of attributes which we have found existing in a number of separate particulars. Thus everything in the notion is borrowed from the particulars ; he who has grasped the particulars has implicitly the notion, for he has all the materials out of which the notion is formed, and when he has developed the notion out of the particulars, he has gained by the process no fresh knowledge ; he has simply rearranged in a more lucid order his old stock of knowledge.

Thus to accuracy of thinking Socrates contributed much, to knowledge he added nothing. But though he did not himself add to the existing store of knowledge, he pointed out the method by which additions might be made—the method of induction, which has been so fruitful in modern times. It is true that he applied his method almost exclusively to moral and political subjects,[1] while he even discouraged the study of physical science, except so far as it directly contributed to human comfort, therein presenting a point of similarity to a very different philosopher, M. Comte. Geometry, he thought, was to be studied so far as it might enable a man to measure land ; astronomy so far as it helped a man to distinguish the time of night, the day of the month, and the time of the year, for such knowledge is useful in travelling, keeping guard, and other occupations. Further study of these sciences he deprecated.[2] It is, however,

---

[1] Σωκράτου δὲ περὶ μὲν τὰ ἠθικὰ πραγματευομένου, περὶ δὲ τῆς ὅλης φύσεως οὐθέν, Arist. Met. 987 b 1, 2. ἐπὶ Σωκράτου δὲ τοῦτο μὲν [scil. τὸ ὁρί-σασθαι τὴν οὐσίαν] ηὐξήθη, τὸ δὲ ζητεῖν τὰ περὶ φύσεως ἔληξε, Arist. Part. An. 642 a 28 sq.; Xen. Mem. i. 1. 11-13.

[2] Xen. Mem. iv. 7.

just in application to the physical sciences that this method has been productive of vast results, and it is a little curious that while in ancient times induction was first applied to moral subjects, and only afterwards to some small extent (as, *e.g.*, in the biological works of Aristotle) to natural science, in modern times the order has been reversed. It was first applied to physical science (as by Bacon and his predecessors as well as successors), and it was not till afterwards that the attempt was made, as by Hume,[1] to apply it to the study of mind. Thus Socrates did great service to philosophy and science by pointing out the principle upon which all human knowledge, which is practically of any use, depends, the principle of generalization. Though by evolving clear general notions out of the confused mass of particulars in the minds of his hearers, he did not, as I have said, add to the stock of their knowledge, yet he prepared the way for such additions. For additions to our knowledge worth the name are not made merely by increasing the sphere of our observation, *i.e.* by supplying us with a fresh store of particulars. A dog may have its knowledge increased to this extent. It is possible that a dog's experience, *i.e.* the amount of particulars which it has observed by sense, may be quite as extensive as that of a man. But man's vastly greater power of generalization enables him from the observation of particulars to infer general laws, which furnish him with knowledge that extends beyond the mere sphere of his observation to the distant in time and space.

It can hardly be too emphatically inculcated that with Socrates generalization was only the road to knowledge, not to existence ; only the way in which we attain a comprehensive view of things, not the way in which things exist. Plato (and Aristotle too) overlooked this. In the joy felt at the great discovery they deified general notions, making our highest form of knowledge the highest form of existence. They overlooked the fact that generalization, while the highest power of the human intellect and a mark of its strength, is no less a mark of its weakness. Generalization is but the compendious and imperfect way in which a finite mind grasps the infinity of particulars. A mind that could grasp at

---

[1] *Treatise of Human Nature*, Introd. p. 308 ed. Greene and Grose.

once all the particulars would not generalize. We say, for example, that " every particle of matter attracts every other with a force varying inversely as the square of the distance ", because it is impossible for us to know the exact amount with which every particle of matter attracts every other in the universe ; but if there is a mind which grasps the totality of things, it, knowing the exact amount of the attraction between each particle of matter in the universe, can have no need to have recourse to the summary which the limitation of our minds compels us to make use of. The knowledge of universals is, as Aristotle says,[1] the nearest approach to full and perfect knowledge of which we are capable ; but still this general knowledge is not a proper knowledge of particulars, it is only knowledge in a certain sense.[2] General knowledge we may call a potential knowledge. In itself it gives us no real knowledge, *i.e.* knowledge of real things, for the only real things are particulars, and general knowledge does not of itself give us any information about them. Thus we could well accept the Aristotelian dogma that in God's thought there is nothing potential, all is actual,[3] if we were to understand by this that God's thought is all of particulars, with no admixture of the imperfection of general notions. (However, Aristotle, in attributing to God actual (not potential) knowledge ($\theta\epsilon\omega\rho\iota a$), had not in view this distinction between the knowledge of universals and that of particulars, but that between knowledge exercised and knowledge dormant.)

Thus the power of forming general notions, while, as the necessary condition of reasoning, it is the strength of the human intellect, is also a badge of its weakness. Winged by this power, our thought can travel on into regions of space where no human eye has penetrated or foot trod ; it can pass back into regions of time when man was not,

---

[1] *Metaph.* A c. 2, 982 b 20 *sqq.*

[2] οὗτος γὰρ [scil. ὁ τὴν καθόλου ἐπιστήμην μάλιστα ἔχων] οἶδέ πως πάντα τὰ ὑποκείμενα.

[3] *Metaph.* A c. 7 ; *Nic. Eth.* x. cc. 7 and 8 ed. Bekker, especially p. 1178 b 21, 22 ἡ τοῦ θέου ἐνεργεία μακαριότητι διαφέρουσα θεωρητικὴ ἂν εἴη. θεωρία which Aristotle attributes to God is, in its Aristotelian sense, actualized as opposed to potential knowledge. Trendelenberg on Arist. *de Anima*, pp. 258-259, 2nd ed. ; *id.* *Elem. Leg. Arist.* § 16, Bonitz Ind. Arist. 329 a 45 *sqq.* ; *id.* 328 a 54 *sqq.* "θεωρεῖν ab ἐπιστήμη perinde distinguitur atque ἐνεργεία a δυνάμει."

and forward into the future when man and the system of
which he is an insignificant member, shall be no more.
But if this power casts a gleam on the distant in space and
time, it equally reveals the darkness, for it shows us what
we do not know, and the unknown is vastly greater than the
known. It thus at once exalts and humbles us ; it reveals
the infinite but reminds us that we ourselves are finite.

Quiesce mens heic denique,	Quod quaeris in te repperis :
Arctosque nosce limites,	In mente sunt, in mente sunt,
Queis contineris undique ;	Hi, quos requiris, termini ;
Quiesce mens, et limites	A rebus absunt limites,
In orbe cessa quaerere.	In hisce tantum infinitas,

Infinitas ! Infinitas !

II

But it is time to turn to Plato, and to attempt to trace
the history of that gigantic and yet splendid error, which
converted a true theory of knowledge into a false theory of
being, which turned, in other words, logic into ontology.

Aristotle [1] tells us that Plato was in his youth familiar
with Cratylus, [2] by whom he was imbued with the Heraclitean
doctrines. Aristotle's words certainly seem to imply, though
they do not distinctly assert, that Plato had studied the
Heraclitean philosophy before he made the acquaintance of
Socrates. It may have been so (and Zeller [3] regards it as
certain), but assuredly in the earlier works of Plato there
is no trace of such influence. The writings of Plato may
be roughly divided into two groups, the Socratic dialogues
and the Platonic. In the former Plato mostly repeats the
doctrines of Socrates, in the latter his own speculations
appear. The second group might perhaps be divided again
into the purely Platonic (containing the Ideal system in its
original form) and the Pythagorean, in which the Ideal
theory was beginning to be assimilated to the numerical
theories of the Pythagoreans. But our information about
this last stage of Platonism is chiefly derived from Aristotle ;

---

[1] *Metaph.* i. c. 6, § 2.
[2] For whom, Zeller, vol. i. p. 675,   4th ed.   [3] *Plato*, p. 9.

and it would be hardly possible to form a group of Pythagorean dialogues, though in some of Plato's later works (especially the *Timaeus* and *Philebus*) there are manifest tokens of the coming change. To the first, the Socratic group, I would assign the dialogues *Hippias Major* and *Minor*, *Ion*, *Euthyphro*, *Laches*, *First Alcibiades* (if genuine, about which I have doubts), *Lysis*, *Charmides*, *Euthydemus*, and *Protagoras*, to which may probably be added the *Crito* and *Apology*. (These last, however, being unphilosophical, do not concern us here.) Now these dialogues are either purely Socratic (the *Hippias Major* and *Minor*, the *Ion*, *Euthyphro*, *Laches*, and *Protagoras*), or Socratic tinged with the coming Platonism (*Lysis*, *Charmides*, *Euthydemus*). There seems to be no trace in these dialogues of the influence of the great physical philosophy of the Pre-Socratic period. It is true that passages in the *Lysis* show that Plato was acquainted with some of these doctrines, probably the Empedoclean,[1] and certainly the Heraclitean.[2] But this proves nothing more than a mere acquaintance with the opinions of these early philosophers; the dialogues themselves are wholly uninfluenced by any such opinions. Plato started completely from the Socratic standpoint ; what he sought was correct general notions. Thus his early dialogues are Socratic both in form and matter. Beauty, which is the subject of the *Hippias Major*, was, we know, discussed by Socrates :[3] piety, the subject of the *Euthyphro*, was a common theme with Socrates :[4] courage, the subject of the *Laches*, was also a theme of Socrates :[5] so with friendship, the subject of the *Lysis*,[6] and temperance, the subject of the *Charmides*.[7] The way in which the Platonic (?) Socrates

[1] *Lysis*, 214 B; Stallbaum thinks that Anaxagoras is here referred to, but see Aristotle, *Nic. Eth.* viii. c. 1, § 6.

[2] *Lysis*, 215 C-E. Of course he was acquainted with the Sophists, Hippias, Protagoras, Prodicus, etc. Prodicus especially seems to have amused Plato, and he is referred to very often. *Euthyd.* 277 E; *Hipp. Maj.* 282; *Laches*, 197 D; *Charm.* 163 D; *Protag.* 337 A-C; *ib.* 340 A *sqq.*; *ib.*

358 A; *ib.* D and E; *Meno*, 75 E; *ib.* 96 D; *Apol.* 19 E; *Theaet.* 151 B; *Crat.* 384 B; *Rep.* 600 C.

[3] Xen. *Mem.* i. 1. 16; iv. 8.

[4] Xen. *Mem.* i. 1. 16; iv. 6. 2-4, and on the relation of gods to men generally *Mem.* i. 4; iv. 3.

[5] Xen. *Mem.* i. 1. 16; iv. 9. 1-3.

[6] Xen. *Mem.* ii. 4, 5, and 6; iii. 11.

[7] Xen. *Mem.* i. 5; ii. 1; iv. 5.

in the *First Alcibiades* convicts Alcibiades of ignorance of
those things which a statesman should know, very much
resembles the mode in which Glaucon, who was similarly
ambitious of taking part in politics, is convicted of a like
ignorance by the Xenophontic Socrates,[1] and equally in
both [Plato] and Xenophon does Socrates insist on that
knowledge of self which the Delphic inscription [2] prescribed.[3]
The *Ion* also contains a characteristically Socratic exposure
of ignorance, and it was quite in Socrates' way to interrogate
people upon their special profession, as here he interrogates
Ion the rhapsodist.[4] The *Protagoras* is the most systematic
exposition which we possess of the doctrine that all particular
moral virtues can be resolved into knowledge, and this we
know was a characteristic doctrine of Socrates.[5] Lastly, the
positive part of the *Euthydemus* [6] consists of a beautiful
exposition of the Socratic doctrine of the supreme importance
of wisdom.

The theme of all these dialogues is that which we saw
to be the central point in the thinking of Socrates—Knowledge.
Sometimes [7] the want of knowledge is exposed, sometimes [8]
the value of it is insisted upon ; sometimes the dialogues
are searches after knowledge, as the *Hippias Major, Euthyphro, Laches, Lysis, Charmides*. Moreover, this knowledge
is sought in correct general notions, and though the search
in these five dialogues is unsuccessful, the negative result is
characteristic of the historical Socrates.[9] A general notion
is sought, and Socrates' respondent begins in some cases by
giving particular instances of the general notion instead of the
general notion itself. Euthyphro gives particular pious acts [10]

---

[1] *Mem.* iii. 6.

[2] To the passages quoted by Liddell
& Scott, *s.v.* γράμμα in which this
inscription is referred to as the
Δελφικὸν γράμμα, etc., I would add
Plato, *Alc. I.* 132 C; *Charm.* 164 D;
Phaedr. 229 E; *Legg.* 923 A; *Rival*,
138 A; and *Phileb.* 48 C (where the
plural γράμματα is used).

[3] Plato, *Alc. I.* 129, etc.; Xen.
Mem. iv. 2. 24-29.

[4] Compare Xen. *Mem.* iii. 10. 1-5,
where Socrates converses with Par-
rhasius the painter ; *ib.* §§ 6-8, with

Cleiton the sculptor ; §§ 9-15, with an
armourer ; *ib.* ch. 11, he converses
with Theodota, a hetaira.

[5] [Arist.] *Nic. Eth.* vi. c. 13, p. 1144
b 17 *sqq.*; iii. c. 11, p. 1116 b 4;
Eud. Eth. i. c. 5, p. 1216 b 2 *sqq.*

[6] The first conversation of Socrates
with Cleinias, 278 E-282 D.

[7] As in the *Ion* and *Alcib. I.*

[8] As in the *Euthyd.* 278 E-282 D;
Lysis, 207 D-210 D.

[9] Arist. *Soph. El.* 183.

[10] P. 5 D.

instead of a general definition of piety ; so Laches in the
case of courage,[1] and most ludicrously of all, Hippias in the
case of beauty.[2] The difficulty experienced by Socrates'
respondents in grasping general notions illustrates the state
of thought at the time that Socrates first turned attention
to the subject, and shows the originality of his method. On
receiving such answers the Platonic Socrates proceeds to
point out that they are inadequate, that while giving some
particulars they leave out many, and he explains that he
wishes to receive an answer which shall include all particulars
whatever. Thus when Euthyphro in answer to the question,
what is piety (τὸ ὅσιον), enumerates several pious acts, Socrates
points out that there are many other pious acts besides
those which Euthyphro has mentioned, and intimates his
wish to hear, not an enumeration of several out of the many
pious acts, but a definition of the general notion of piety.[3]
Thus prompted, Euthyphro rises to the occasion, and pro-
pounds a definition which is general. His definition, however
(" that which is pleasing to the gods ", or modified, " that
which is pleasing to all the gods "), is shown to be untenable.
By way of helping to a definition Socrates [4] suggests the
connexion of the general notion of piety with the general
notion of justice ; and this gives him an opportunity of
illustrating the relation of genus to species, i.e. of the more
general notion to the less general which it includes. He
points out (against Stasinus) that fear is a more general
notion than reverence, that the latter is a species of the former,
since wherever there is reverence there is fear, but where
there is fear there is not always reverence.[5] Again Even
(τὸ ἄρτιον) is a species of the genus number. So piety
(Euthyphro concludes) is a species of the more general
notion of justice.[6] The genus justice is, he thinks, divided

---

[1] P. 190 E.

[2] Hipp. Maj. 287 E-293 D.

[3] αὐτὸ τὸ εἶδος ᾧ πάντα τὰ ὅσια ὅσιά
ἐστιν· ἔφησθα γάρ που μιᾷ ἰδέᾳ τά τε
ἀνοσία ἀνόσια εἶναι καὶ τὰ ὅσια ὅσια.—
ταύτην τοίνυν με αὐτὴν δίδαξον τὴν ἰδέαν,
τίς ποτέ ἐστιν, ἵνα εἰς ἐκείνην ἀποβλέπων
καὶ χρώμενος αὐτῇ παραδείγματι ὃ μὲν
ἂν τοιοῦτον ᾖ, ὧν ἂν σὺ ἢ ἄλλος τις

πράττῃ, φῶ ὅσιον εἶναι, ὃ δ' ἂν μὴ
τοιοῦτον, μὴ φῶ, p. 6 D, E. The use of
the words εἶδος, ἰδέα and παράδειγμα
here is to be noticed.

[4] P. 11 E.

[5] c. 13.

[6] The word used for species is in
these cases μόριον and μέρος, p. 12
C, D.

into two species, one of these being the justice which relates to the gods (and this is piety), the other the species which relates to men.[1]

In a similar manner when Laches answers the question, what is courage? by giving a particular brave act,[2] Socrates shows that there are many other brave acts, and that he wishes an answer which will include them all, and he illustrates his meaning by defining the general notion swiftness. He points out that the species of swiftness are many, but that all these species are included in the general notion of "power which effects much in a short time".[3] Laches then gives a general definition, but Socrates shows that it errs on the opposite side ; while the first definition was too particular, the second is too general, and hence includes more than courage. So Hippias, when asked for a definition of beauty, replies by naming particular beautiful things ; beauty is, he thinks, a beautiful girl,[4] or gold,[5] or it consists in being rich, healthy, and honoured by the Greeks, in living to a good old age, in burying one's parents honourably, and in being buried honourably oneself.[6] Socrates exposes the folly of these answers, and leads the way to general definitions. From these bunglers Charmides is honourably distinguished in that, being asked to define temperance (σωφροσύνη), he at once gives a general definition[7] instead of a number of particular cases. This, along with other points, seems to me an indication that the *Charmides* is one of the later dialogues of the Socratic period. Various other general definitions of temperance are afterwards attempted.[8]

With the special matter of these dialogues I am not concerned. All that I wish to indicate is that they are attempts to reach knowledge by the method of forming general notions, and that these general notions are still regarded simply as the forms in which we know, not as

---

[1] P. 12 E.

[2] *Laches*, p. 190 E.

[3] τὴν ἐν ὀλίγῳ χρόνῳ πολλὰ διαπραττομένην δύναμιν ταχυτῆτα ἔγωγε καλῶ καὶ περὶ φωνὴν καὶ περὶ δρόμον καὶ περὶ τἆλλα πάντα, p. 192 B.

[4] P. 288 E.

[5] P. 289 E.

[6] P. 291 D, E.

[7] Viz. that temperance is ἡσυχιότης τις, p. 159 B.

[8] That it is αἰδώς, that it is τὸ τὰ ἑαυτοῦ πράττειν, that it is τὸ γιγνώσκειν αὐτὸν ἑαυτόν.

forms in which things exist. Therefore, that this method
should be applied (as it is in the Socratic dialogues of Plato)
chiefly to moral subjects, does not concern us, though we
may note in passing that the Socratic doctrine of the
resolution of all virtues into knowledge is distinctly, though
covertly, maintained in the *Laches* and *Protagoras*, and
indicated, though less clearly, in the *Charmides* and *Euthydemus*. The *Laches* sets out with an attempt to discover
the special virtue courage, and ends by discovering that
courage is inseparable from universal virtue, which is found
to consist in an universal knowledge of good and evil.[1]
Thus whether we regard the matter or the method of these
dialogues, we see that their key-note is the key-note of
the Socratic philosophy—knowledge, and knowledge of universals. (I may notice that the *Hippias Minor* contains an
excellent example of the Socratic induction,[2] where the
examples are drawn from ordinary life, as we know was
the practice of Socrates.[3] This induction in the *Hippias
Minor* would be one proof, if proof were needed, of the
genuineness of that dialogue. But the whole piece is
thoroughly Platonic, and is besides supported by a reference
of Aristotle.[4]) So far then all is purely Socratic ; knowledge,
and mainly moral knowledge, is alone treated of ; of the
later Platonic ontology as of the earlier physical philosophy
there is as yet no trace.

I have said, however, that some of the Socratic dialogues,
while uninfluenced by the previous physical philosophy,
are yet tinged by a kind of anticipation of those peculiarly
Platonic doctrines which in the second group of dialogues
are developed into prominence. The dialogues which ex-
hibit this tincture most strongly, and which accordingly
are probably the latest dialogues of the Socratic period,
are the *Charmides*, *Lysis*, and *Euthydemus*. It is true
that all through the dialogues of this first period we may

---

[1] Cp. *Laches*, p. 199 D, E.

[2] Pp. 373 D-375.

[3] Xen. *Mem.* i. 2. 37 ἀλλὰ τῶνδέ
τοί σε ἀπέχεσθαι, ἔφη, δεήσει, ὦ
Σώκρατες, τῶν σκυτέων καὶ τῶν τεκτόνων
καὶ τῶν χαλκέων· καὶ γὰρ οἶμαι αὐτοὺς
ἤδη κατατετρῖφθαι διαθρυλουμένους ὑπὸ

σοῦ : in Plato's *Sympos.* p. 221 E Alcibiades describes the λόγοι of Socrates :
ὄνους γὰρ καὶ κανθήλους λέγει καὶ
χαλκέας τινὰς καὶ σκυτοτόμους καὶ
βυρσοδέψας, καὶ ἀεὶ διὰ τῶν αὐτῶν ταὐτὰ
φαίνεται λέγειν.

[4] *Metaph.* Δ c. 29, p. 1025 a 6 *sqq.*

detect special points of resemblance to peculiarities of opinion or manner which appear more distinctly in the later works.   But these are special points, not affecting the Platonic doctrine as a whole, or at least that aspect of it with which we are here concerned.   As instances of such points of agreement, I may cite in the *Euthydemus* the opinion that the popular legends of the gods were immoral in their tendency ; [1] in the *Laches* [2] the opinion that for some men it is better to die than to live ; hence that an art such as medicine or seamanship, which saves life, is not simply on that account good ; [3] in the *Charmides* [4] the principle of the division of labour is hinted at which is afterwards carried out in the *Republic* ; [5] in the *Euthydemus* [6] and *Protagoras* [7] the question of the teachability of virtue, which is afterwards discussed in the *Meno*, is broached ; in the same dialogue [8] the same view is taken of the function of politics which is afterwards maintained at length in the *Gorgias*, only that in the *Gorgias* virtue takes the place of knowledge ;   the same view of punishment is taken in the *Protagoras* [9] that is afterwards stated in the *Gorgias* ; [10] the view of the effect which music has upon character expressed in *Protagoras* [11] is exactly the same with that expressed at greater length in the *Republic* ; [12] in the same dialogue [13] the same objection to written discourse is made incidentally which is drawn out in the *Phaedrus* ; [14] the notion of the madness of poets appears in the *Ion* ; [15] in the *Lysis* [16] as later in the *Symposium*,[17] the philosopher is described as midway between the wise and the ignorant.   But it is needless to multiply instances of agreement on such special points.   It is more important to notice that in two of the dialogues which I have assigned to the Socratic period, the *Lysis* and the *Euthydemus*, there is a foreshadowing of

---

[1] *Euthydemus*, pp. 5 E-6 A, cp. *Rep.*
ii. p. 377 B-iii. p. 391 E.
[2] P. 195 C, D, etc.
[3] Cp. *Gorgias*, pp. 511, 512.
[4] P. 161 E.
[5] Pp. 370 *sqq.*
[6] P. 282 B, C.
[7] Pp. 319 A-320 B.
[8] P. 292 B.
[9] P. 324 A and B.

[10] P. 525 A, etc.
[11] P. 326 B.
[12] Pp. 400 C-402 A.
[13] *Protag.* p. 329.
[14] P. 275 D.
[15] P. 533 E ; cp. *Phaedrus*, p. 245 A ; *ib.* p. 265 B.
[16] P. 218 A, B.
[17] Pp. 203 E-204 B.

that ontological theory which in the second stage of Plato's thought took the place of, or engrafted itself on, the logical. Such a foreshadowing can hardly be found in the *Charmides*, in the discussion which we find there on the nature of relation.[1] It is there found that the existence of some relative things (*e.g.* quantity) is certain, and the existence of anything absolute, *i.e.* out of all relations to anything but itself, is extremely doubtful. Whether there is an absolute, and, if there be, whether knowledge or a particular kind of knowledge is absolute, is left an open question. It would be a mistake to imagine that Plato, in writing thus about an absolute, had thought out his theory of absolute being, or ideas. In the *Lysis*[2] it is said that something is dear (φίλον) to us for the sake of something else ; that something else is also dear, and it must be so for the sake of something else which is dear, and that something else for the sake of something else, and so on till we come to something which is primarily dear, which is the cause of every other lower member in the series being dear, but which is not itself dear for the sake of anything else.[3] Reading this by the light of later Platonism, we can easily see the resemblance between the πρῶτον φίλον which makes all things else φίλα, and the αὐτὸ τὸ καλόν by participation in which all the καλά are καλά, but there can be little doubt that the ideal theory had not dawned on Plato when he wrote the *Lysis*. (I may note in passing the confusion produced in this dialogue by the double sense of φίλος -η -ον ; the word has both an active sense = loving, friendly; and a passive = loved, dear. Both are mixed up in the dialogue.) In the *Euthydemus*,[4] Zeller[5] and Stallbaum[6] find an enunciation of the ideal theory. The Sophist Dionysodorus asks Socrates whether there is any difference between beauty (τὸ καλόν) and beautiful things (καλὰ πράγματα). Socrates replies that there is ; beautiful things are different from beauty, but are beautiful by the

---

[1] Pp. 167 B-169 B.
[2] c. 15.
[3] ἆρ' οὖν οὐκ ἀνάγκη ἀπειπεῖν ἡμᾶς οὕτως ἰόντας, καὶ ἀφικέσθαι ἐπί τινα ἀρχὴν ἣ οὐκέτ' ἐπανοίσει ἐπ' ἄλλο φίλον, ἀλλ' ἥξει ἐπ' ἐκεῖνο, ὃ ἐστι πρῶτον

φίλον, οὗ ἕνεκα καὶ τᾶλλά φαμεν πάντα φίλα εἶναι; ἀνάγκη, p. 219 C, D.
[4] Pp. 300 E-301 B.
[5] P. 126, note 80.
[6] Proleg. to *Euthydemus*, p. 41 ; *id.* Proleg. to *Cratylus*, p. 25.

presence of a certain beauty.[1] This notion of a thing
becoming so and so by the presence of something else is
then ridiculed by the Sophist. I can hardly agree with
Zeller that this is a distinct enunciation of the ideal doctrine.
The passage might have been written by Plato in his Socratic
stage, when he had simply learned to distinguish the universal from the particular, without yet giving the universal
an objective existence, though the passage indicates a sort
of transition to or preparation for the later stage.

III

The early works which have been discussed were written,
I conceive, at various times in the interval of ten or twelve
years which elapsed between the death of Socrates and the
time when Plato established himself as a teacher at Athens,
and perhaps before he travelled in Cyrene, Egypt, Sicily,
and Italy. With them the first epoch in the intellectual life
of Plato is at an end ; the first act is over, and when the
curtain again rises, the scene is changed. Plato returned from
his travels with larger experience and widened views, and
the result is seen in the great change in his views. The
result of my inquiry into this change may perhaps be best
expressed in the words of Plato himself : [2] τελευτῶν οὕτως
ἐμαυτῷ ἔδοξα πρὸς ταύτην τὴν σκέψιν ἀφυὴς εἶναι ὡς οὐδὲν
χρῆμα. τεκμήριον δέ σοι ἐρῶ ἱκανόν· ἐγὼ γὰρ ἃ καὶ πρότερον σαφῶς ἠπιστάμην, ὥς γε ἐμαυτῷ ἐδόκουν, τότε ὑπὸ
ταύτης τῆς σκέψεως οὕτω σφόδρα ἐτυφλώθην, ὥστε ἀπέμαθον
καὶ ταῦτα ἃ πρὸ τοῦ ᾤμην εἰδέναι. With this admission, I
am, however, forced to proceed with the subject, and attempt
to make something out of it.

One feature in which some of the later dialogues differ
from those of the first period is that they lead to affirmative conclusions. The negative dialectic which we associate
with Socrates has been to a great extent abandoned. This
marks an advance beyond the Socratic standpoint. In
respect of doctrine again, the great feature of the second
group is the Ideal theory which reigns supreme in Plato's

---

[1] ἕτερα ἔφην [τὰ καλὰ] αὐτοῦ γε τοῦ   κάλλος τι.
καλοῦ· πάρεστι μέντοι ἑκάστῳ αὐτῶν   [2] *Phaedo*, p. 96 C.

greatest works, and is only abandoned (if at all) in his latest writings. Over the tone, too, of the dialogues a change has come. It is solemn, often sombre, and deepens at times into sadness. As this feeling grows, the humour becomes more and more subdued and finally disappears altogether. Amongst these later dialogues the *Theaetetus* possesses two features which might seem to connect it with the earlier writings ; its result is negative, and the Ideal theory (though hinted at) does not distinctly appear in it. But it is undoubtedly one of the mature works of Plato, and is well fitted to serve as an introduction to the Ideal theory, and with this end in view Plato seems to have produced it. The earlier dialogues are searches after knowledge or rather after particular knowledges (if I may be allowed the expression, an old English one, I believe, and very useful) ; the *Theaetetus* is a search after knowledge in general. The *Theaetetus* investigates sensation and decides that knowledge consists neither in sensation by itself nor in sensations (or their images preserved by memory) combined into judgement. The whole aim of the *Theaetetus* is to prepare for a proof that knowledge is innate in the reason, not acquired by sense experience, and that its true objects are not the data of sense but a world of supersensuous realities. The *Theaetetus* breaks down the " bridge of fancies " (as Plato deemed it) which links us to the lower world, and henceforward turning his back resolutely on the broken bridge, Plato sets himself patiently to grope his way upward to the world above. If this view of the *Theaetetus* as an introduction to the Ideal theory be correct, it matters little to what year we assign its composition. The passage usually appealed to for determining the date is the introduction,[1] in which Theaetetus is said to have been wounded in a battle, and to be at the port of Megara (Nisaea) on his way from Corinth to Athens. The critics try to fix the date of the dialogue by determining the date of the battle here alluded to ; it has been referred to 394, 390 (or a few years later), and 368. It is hardly necessary to observe that even if we knew for certain the date of the battle, this would not give us the date of the dialogue ; it would only tell us the year before which

[1] P. 142.

the dialogue (or at least the part which contains the mention of the battle) could not have been written. Certainly I cannot think that the dialogue was written about 394 B.C. The nature of the contents points to some time between 390 and 380, the time when Plato established himself as a teacher at Athens, and began to expound his doctrine of Ideas. On the other hand, certain circumstances seem to make for a considerably later date. The dialogue is connected dramatically with the *Sophist* and *Politicus*, and these I take to be late dialogues, later probably than the *Republic*. Now internal evidence seems to show that the *Republic* was written between 382 and 371. Supposing, then, the *Sophist* and *Politicus* to be later than the *Republic*, and the *Theaetetus* to have been written about the same time, the date 368 would tally well enough. But in making use of the allusion to the battle as a means for helping to fix the date of the *Theaetetus*, there is this difficulty, that the introduction [1] is wholly distinct from the rest of the dialogue, and might quite well have been composed at a different time. And the dramatic union of the *Theaetetus*, *Sophist*, and *Politicus* by no means proves that these works were composed at the same time. Yet some points are in favour of the later date. Thus in *Theaetetus* [2] and *Sophist* [3] there are allusions to a conversation held between Socrates in his youth and the aged Parmenides. Now this conversation may perhaps be more naturally referred to Plato's dialogue *Parmenides* than to a real conversation between Socrates and Parmenides. The references agree very exactly.[4] Now if these passages in the *Theaetetus* and *Sophist* really refer to the dialogue *Parmenides*, then the dialogues themselves must have been written later than it. But the contents of the *Parmenides*, especially its searching criticism of the Ideal theory, makes the lateness of its composition almost unquestionable. Still later, therefore, must have been the *Theaetetus* and *Sophist*. There

---

[1] Pp. 142 A-143 C.
[2] P. 183 E.
[3] P. 217 E.
[4] In the *Parmenides* it is said of the Eleatic philosopher that εὖ μάλα ἤδη πρεσβύτην εἶναι, σφόδρα πολιόν. Cp. *Soph. l.c,* ἐκείνου (*scil,* Παρμενίδου)

μάλα δὴ τότε ὄντος πρεσβύτου, *cf. Theaet. l.c.* πάνυ πρεσβύτῃ: in the *Parm.* Socrates is very young, Σωκράτη δὲ εἶναι τότε σφόδρα νέον, p. 127 C ; *cf. Soph. l.c.* ἐγὼ νέος ὤν, *Theaet. l.c.* πάνυ νέος,

are other points of similarity between the dialogues. The definition in *Theaetetus* [1] of τὸ διανοεῖσθαι and of δόξα correspond clearly to those in the *Sophist*. [2] Again the hint in the *Theaetetus* [3] that Plato holds a position intermediate between the Eleatics and Heracliteans reminds us of the way in which he treats two opposite schools in the *Sophist*. But stronger perhaps than arguments from particular circumstances is the argument from the general style of the language in the *Theaetetus, Sophist,* and *Politicus*. The smooth and flowing style in which the dialogues of the first and those of the earlier part of the second period are written was exchanged in Plato's later life for a hard and angular one, suggestive not (as the earlier dialogues) of wave succeeding wave, but of solid blocks fitted laboriously into each other. Of the former, the flowing style, the most brilliant examples are the *Protagoras, Gorgias, Phaedo,* and *Symposium,* and to this class may be referred (along with many lesser dialogues including all the Socratic) the *Phaedrus* and *Republic,* but in these two latter the flow is by no means so smooth ; in the *Republic* especially jolts are not uncommon. Of the second, the stumping or halting style, the *Timaeus, Sophist, Politicus,* and *Philebus* are the most undoubted examples, though the sound of the wooden leg (if I may say so) is not so painfully obvious in the *Sophist* and *Politicus* as in the other two. (The *Laws* would probably have formed another of this group ; but the text was left in too imperfect a state at Plato's death to enable us to pass a judgement on the form which it might finally have taken in his hands.) The *Republic* seems to have been the turning-point between the two styles. I am inclined to class the *Theaetetus* in point of style with the *Sophist, Politicus,* etc., rather than with the *Phaedo, Symposium,* etc. If I am right in this, it forms a strong argument for the late date of the *Theaetetus.* For it would be strange if the series of dialogues written in the smooth style were interrupted by one written in the stiff style into which Plato fell in later years. To this it might be objected that the *Parmenides* (a late dialogue) is written in the smooth style, and if Plato

---

[1] Pp. 189 E-190 A.
[2] Pp. 263 E-264 A. Cp. too *Phileb.* p. 38 B-E.
[3] Pp. 180 E-181 A.

could change his style in the one case, he might have done it in the other. But leaving the question of the date (which is after all unimportant), it is necessary to see more exactly how the *Theaetetus* prepares for the ideal theory.

The general notions which Socrates aimed at grasping were derived from particulars, and these particulars were (in many cases at least) given by sense. In the Socratic dialogues Plato had pursued the generalizing process without examining the foundations on which it rests, without, in other words, considering particulars and the mode in which they are presented to us by sense. The *Theaetetus* attempts to supply this deficiency. It goes back to the particulars of sense, and inquires whether all our knowledge is supplied by the senses—whether knowledge is sensation. The whole dialogue is thus subjective; it deals essentially with our faculties of knowing, only incidentally with the objects of knowledge, differing herein from those dialogues in which the objects of knowledge (viz. the Ideas) are all-important and our faculties of knowledge are nearly overlooked. The dialogue is divided into three main parts. In the first, knowledge is defined by Theaetetus as sensation;[1] in the second, it is defined as true opinion;[2] in the third as true opinion μετὰ λόγου, *i.e.* in conjunction with an explanation or definition (though what exactly this λόγος is, not the interlocutors themselves can agree upon). But δόξα is (as I shall point out) only sense knowledge transformed; it is simply judgement exercised on the data of sense. Thus sensation is the subject of the dialogue throughout. The inadequacy of mere sensation to account for all our knowledge was perceived by Plato as clearly perhaps as by Kant.

I have already indicated[3] the state of mind to which we would be reduced were we possessed only of the powers of sensation. It may be well to draw out a little more in detail some of the consequences which follow from the supposition that sensation is co-extensive with knowledge and to show that Plato was fully aware of them. In the first place sensation is only of the present; had we nothing but sensation, memory

---

[1] After he had first made the old error of giving an enumeration of particulars instead of a general definition. cc. 8-30.
[2] cc. 31-38.
[3] Pp. 3 and 4.

and expectation would be alike impossible ; we would be shut out from the distant in time, and limited to the present moment. (This consequence, so far as memory is concerned, is stated in *Theaetetus*.¹ It is true that in the latter passages of the *Theaetetus* Plato is combating not directly the doctrine propounded by Theaetetus that knowledge is sensation, but the Protagorean doctrine that man is the measure of all things, that what seems true to a man is true to him. But the two doctrines in Plato's opinion coincide.²) An immediate consequence of this is that personal identity is lost. Personal identity depends upon memory ; memory is the chain which binds our past experience in that unity which constitutes self. If we had nothing but the present sensation we would not be conscious that we had existed the moment before ; from ourself of the previous moment we would be separated as completely as we are at present from the self of any person other than ourselves. Thus we should not be one person but a succession of distinct persons succeeding each other in time with inconceivable rapidity.³ Compared with such fleeting lives, the life of an insect of a day would seem an age.

Again, if we were limited wholly to sensation, our different sensations even when simultaneous would be wholly unconnected ; we could not compare or contrast them by mere sensation, since a sensation stands alone and can give no information about anything but itself. By mere sensation we could neither compare the different sensations of any one sense (say the colours blue and red given by sight), nor the different sensations of different senses (say the blue given by sight and the sound of the waves given by hearing).⁴ Thus

---

¹ Pp. 163 C-164 D, and so far as expectation is concerned, *ib.* pp. 171 E-172 B, 177 C-179 C. Cp. *Philebus*, p. 21 C.

² *Theaet.* pp. 151 E-152 A and 160 D.

³ *Theaet.* p. 166 B δοκεῖς τινά σοι
. . . δώσειν ποτὲ τὸν αὐτὸν εἶναι τὸν ἀνομοιούμενον τῷ πρὶν ἀνομοιοῦσθαι ὄντι; μᾶλλον δὲ τὸν εἶναί τινα, ἀλλ' οὐχὶ τούς, καὶ τούτους γιγνομένους ἀπείρους, ἐάνπερ ἀνομοίωσις γίγνηται. The loss

of personal identity, however, is here viewed not as arising from want of memory, but from actual ἀνομοίωσις, *i.e.* the subject becomes really different every moment that it meets with a different object ; each modifies the other, their products are always different. But the result is the same from whichever point of view we look at it.

⁴ Cp. *Theaet.* pp. 184 B *sqq.* For the comparison of the different sensations

would our mind lose its unity not only (as we have seen) of succession but also of simultaneity. Not only would the mind be really a succession of totally distinct minds, but even at one and the same moment of time it would not be one mind but really as many minds as there happened to be simultaneous sensations, for each of these sensations would be totally distinct from and unconnected with all the others. What we call mind would resemble (to use Plato's own illustration) the Trojan horse ; it would be really a plurality of minds which, though outwardly connected, had no mental union.[1]

An immediate consequence of this would be that we could have no perception of what we call things. The notion we form of a thing is a combination of various sensations which we have at various times experienced simultaneously. The notion I have of my hand has arisen in some such way as this. At a certain moment the sense of sight gives me the perception of a certain patch of whitish colour of a certain configuration, lying, say, on a green ground. At the same moment, following upon an exertion of will, I am conscious of a muscular sensation of motion, and simultaneously the white patch of colour changes its position on my field of vision while the green ground remains unaltered. Accordingly, I associate these sensations of motion and the patch of whitish colour and the change in the position of the whitish patch. By repeated experiences, by finding that a similar muscular sensation is often accompanied by a similar sensation of sight (that, namely, of a whitish colour changing its position), I come firmly to connect in my mind these two distinct sensations given by the two distinct senses (the muscular sense and the sense of sight), and the notion of these sensations as mutually connected is the notion I have of my hand. (There are of course other sensations which go to make up the group of sensations I call my hand. I have only indicated two of the chief sensations for the sake of illustration.) It is obvious

---

of different senses, *ib.* p. 185 A, B ; for the comparison of different sensations of the same sense, *ib.* p. 185 B, C.

[1] *Theaet.* p. 184 D δεινὸν γάρ που, ὦ παῖ, εἰ πολλαί τινες ἐν ἡμῖν, ὥσπερ ἐν

δουρείοις ἵπποις, αἰσθήσεις ἐγκάθηνται, ἀλλὰ μὴ εἰς μίαν τινὰ ἰδέαν, εἴτε ψυχὴν εἴτε ὅ τι δεῖ καλεῖν, πάντα ταῦτα ξυντείνει, ᾗ διὰ τούτων οἷον ὀργάνων αἰσθανόμεθα ὅσα αἰσθητά.

that at first I could have no reason to expect that the muscular sensation of motion would be followed by any change in the sensations of vision ; or even if I could have been forewarned that such change would take place, I could not have anticipated (in the case supposed) whether the change would be in the white or in the green colour ; if I had been told that one of these colours represented a part of myself called my hand, I could not, before the experience I have described, have said whether it was the white or the green colour that represented my hand, or (more generally) which of all the colours on my field of vision represented my hand.   I might have fixed on the sun or moon just as probably (perhaps more so) as on my hand ; and if I had experienced pain in my hand before I had received the power of moving it, I would have been just as likely to refer the pain to a tree or a house or a stone (*i.e.* to any of the patches of colour on my field of vision) as to my hand.

The case is similar with all the objects we call things. The notion of each is a combination of various sensations which we have frequently experienced simultaneously or in immediate succession.   The notion of a table is a combination of the sensations of colour and shape (received by sight) with the sensations of touch and resistance ; all which sensations have been at times experienced simultaneously. After the notion has been once formed, it is not of course necessary to its excitation in our minds that we should experience simultaneously all the sensations which unite to form it ; one of the sensations may be enough. *E.g.* the notion of a table is excited in our minds by the mere sense of sight.   But though we do not in this case come in contact with the table and thereby experience the sensation of resistance, we yet believe that by going through certain intermediate processes we would experience a sensation of resistance simultaneously with the perception by sight of the colour and figure of the table.   The table is, in short, for us a group not necessarily of actual sensations, but of (in the language of Mill) permanent possibilities of sensation.

Having thus indicated briefly what we mean by things, the truth of the remark made above—that with nothing but sensation we could have no conception of things—will be clearer. Things are groups of distinct sensations of different senses regarded as bound together. But each sense gives only its own sensations ; it cannot view the sensations of other senses in connexion with its own ; it cannot, therefore, be sense that unifies the data of the various senses by binding them together in the bundles we call things ; some power distinct from sense is necessary to effect this unification.[1] Things, Plato saw, are but *groups* of sensations.[2] Just as little can mere sensation give us the aesthetic notions of beauty and ugliness,[3] for these are complex, involving a comparison of notions ; but sensation is simple and is incapable of comparing. Beauty is a " mixed mode " in the language of Locke,[4] *i.e.* it is a doubly complex notion, for even a simple " mode " is a complex idea. Nor, of course, can mere sensation give the moral notions of good and evil.[5]

Thus we see, and Plato saw, the mental state to which we would be reduced had we nothing but sensations. Without knowledge of the past or future, without knowledge of things, we would be but series of totally distinct sensations unconnected either in succession or in simultaneity. Such a life, as Plato says,[6] would be the life not of a man, but of a shellfish. But this is not the state of our minds, therefore our minds must be something more than bundles of senses. We know that we can compare the different sensations given by the same sense [7] and the sensations given by different senses.[8] We say that these sensations are or exist, that they are different from each other, identical with themselves, that they are like and unlike, that they are one, two, three, etc. Now all these notions of existence, difference, sameness, likeness, unlikeness, number, as well as those of beauty and ugliness, goodness and badness, involving as they do (except perhaps the first, that of existence) comparison, cannot have been given by sense. There is thus a power

[1] *Theaet.* pp. 185-186 B.

[2] δεῖ δὲ καὶ κατὰ μέρος οὕτω λέγειν [*i.e.* such is the method of production of each particular sensation] καὶ περὶ πολλῶν ἀθροισθέντων ᾧ δὴ ἀθροίσματι ἄνθρωπόν τε τίθενται καὶ λίθον καὶ ἕκαστον ζῷόν τε καὶ εἶδος, *Theaet.*

p. 157 B, C.

[3] *Theaet.* p. 186 C.

[4] *Essay*, bk. ii. c. 12, § 5.

[5] *Theaet.* p. 186 A.

[6] *Philebus*, p. 21 C.

[7] *Theaet.* p. 185 B, C.

[8] *Id.* p. 185 A, B.

higher than sense which can compare the data of the different
senses, and which furnishes us with notions which we could
never have had if we had been endowed with no mental
powers but the senses. This power which gives unity to
the disconnected data of sense we may call the pure reason.[1]

This, then, is the answer which Plato made to the philosophy
of experience, the philosophy which believes that sensation
alone can account for all our knowledge ; and the passage
in which he makes this reply [2] is one of the most remarkable
in ancient philosophy ; for the answer is substantially
identical, I believe, with the famous one which Kant made
to the sensational philosophy of Locke, as that philosophy
appeared in its full development in the scepticism of Hume.
Several of Kant's categories (*i.e.* the pure notions given by
the reason independent of experience) are identical with
the notions to which Plato here points as not accountable
for by sense.

Plato then proceeds to point out to Theaetetus that the
object of their search, knowledge, must be sought not in
sensation, but in the notions of the reason. Sense, not
giving us the notion of existence, cannot, he thinks, give us
truth. For truth and therefore for knowledge we must
look to the source which gives us the notion of existence,
i.e. to the mind or reason. Sensation then is not knowledge ;
knowledge must be sought for in the operations of the
reason apart from sense.[3] Here then we have the real
conclusion of the *Theaetetus*, the highest point reached in
the discussion,[4] and to this point a modern philosopher may
follow Plato, for these pure notions which he has reached
are still treated by him solely as notions, as forms of knowledge, not of external existence. It is only when he begins
(as we shall see presently) to project these internal forms
on the external world, to realize (χωρίζειν in Aristotelian
language) his ideas, that we must part company from him.

Having thus extracted what seems to be the kernel (at

---

[1] αὐτὴ ἡ ψυχή, *Theaet.* p. 186 B.

[2] *Theaet.* pp. 184 B-187 A.

[3] *Theaet.* pp. 186 C-187 A. The conclusion is ὥστε μὴ ζητεῖν αὐτὴν ἐν
αἰσθήσει τὸ παράπαν ἀλλ' ἐν ἐκείνῳ

τῷ ὀνόματι ὅ τι ποτ' ἔχει ἡ ψυχή, ὅταν
αὐτὴ καθ' αὑτὴν πραγματεύηται περὶ
τὰ ὄντα.

[4] ὅμως δὲ τοσοῦτόν γε προβεβήκαμεν,
as Plato says, *Theaet.* p. 187 A.

least for my purpose) of the *Theaetetus*, I shall not discuss the latter portion of the dialogue in which knowledge is at first identified with true opinion,[1] and afterwards with true opinion μετὰ λόγου. For opinion (in Plato's mind) was essentially a product of sensation ; and the foundation being thus destroyed, the superstructure must fall with it.[2]

But in an attempt to understand the Ideal theory, it would be wrong to leave the *Theaetetus* without taking with us a conception of Plato's view of sensation and the mode of its production, views which he nowhere states with such precision as in the *Theaetetus*. Sensation on the physiological side is treated of at length in the *Timaeus* ;[3] but for sensation on its metaphysical side the *Theaetetus* is all-important. It is true that the theory of sensation here developed depends upon the Heraclitean doctrine of flux, but there is no doubt that Plato accepted this doctrine fully in regard to the sensible world. Neither in the *Theaetetus* nor anywhere else does he, in this respect, attempt to refute it ; and it is accordingly an error in Bonitz[4] to speak of the refutation (*Widerlegung*) by Plato in the *Theaetetus* of the Heraclitean doctrine of flux. Even if the writings of Plato himself left any doubt

---

[1] cc. 31-38.

[2] Though it would perhaps be more suitable to discuss δόξα when we come to the *Republic*, yet as my survey of that dialogue is necessarily very brief, it may be well to state shortly some of the leading points in Plato's doctrine of δόξα. For δόξα compare (besides *Theaetetus*, p. 187 A to end of dialogue) *Meno*, c. 38, pp. 96 E-98 C ; *Soph.* cc. 45, 46, 47, pp. 261 C-264 B ; *Rep.* v. cc. 20-22, pp. 475 C-480 A ; *ib.* vi. c. 20, pp. 509 C-511 E ; vii. pp. 533 D-534 D ; *Phileb.* c. 23, pp. 38 B-39 E ; *ib.* pp. 58 E-59 D ; *Tim.* pp. 51 D-52 A ; *Phaedo*, p. 96 B. Opinion, δόξα, is a product of sensation and memory, ἐκ μνήμης τε καὶ αἰσθήσεως δόξα ἡμῖν καὶ τὸ διαδοξάζειν ἐγχειρεῖν γίγνεθ' ἑκάστοτε, *Phileb.* p. 38, B, C. Cp. *Phaedo*, ἐκ τούτων δὲ [*scil.* τῶν αἰσθήσεων] γίγνοιτο μνήμη καὶ δόξα (*Phaedo*, p. 96 B, where, however, this is only given as a problematical solution of

a difficulty). It consists in a mental affirmation or negation and is thus the conclusion of a mental dialogue (*Soph.* pp. 263 E-264 A). It differs subjectively from knowledge in that it gives facts without giving their causes, and in that it is not permanent (*Meno*, p. 98 A) ; it differs objectively from knowledge, in that the object of opinion is the sensible world, which is always changing, becoming and perishing, while the object of knowledge is the Ideal world, the unbegotten, imperishable, and unchangeable (*Tim.* p. 52 A ; *Rep. ll.cc.* ; *Phil.* pp. 58 E-59 D). Opinion is produced by persuasion), knowledge by instruction ; the former can be altered by persuasion, the latter cannot ; the latter can give a reason for itself, the former cannot (*Tim.* p. 51 E).

[3] c. xvi. and cc. xxvii.-xxx.

[4] *Platonische Studien*, p. 53.

on the subject, such a doubt would be removed by the direct
testimony of Aristotle.[1] Accordingly we may accept the
account of sensation given in the *Theaetetus* as the genuine
view of Plato.[2] The theory is this. In the physical world
there exists nothing but motion. Of motion there are two
kinds, an active and a passive. These, though mentally dis-
tinguishable, arc really inseparable ; the one has no existence
without the other. These motions work together, they are
coefficients, and their product is double, viz. sensations
(αἰσθήσεις) and objects of sensation (αἰσθητά), or in other
words, Perception and the Perceived. The essence of these
products (τὰ γεννώμενα) as well as of their producers (τὰ
γεννῶντα) is motion ; but there is this distinction, that the
motion of the producers is slow, that of the products is swift.
Thus the producers, *i.e.* the active and passive motions (what
we would call object and subject), after approaching within a
certain distance of each other, remain in their places, whilst
between them there passes a double motion, one from the
Agent τὸ ποιοῦν (the Object) to the Patient τὸ πάσχον (the
Subject), the other from the Patient (Subject) to the Agent
(Object). The products of this union of motions are (*a*) sensations, αἰσθήσεις ; (*b*) objects of sensation, αἰσθητά, the
former being the product of the motion from Patient to
Agent, the latter of the motion from Agent to Patient. Thus
colour, which is an αἰσθητόν, is neither something outside
the eyes nor something in the eyes ; it has in fact no place
at all, being but the product of a motion impinging on the
eye.[3] So with all sensations of hardness, heat, etc., they are
not anything absolute, do not exist by themselves ; they are
all produced by the union of two motions.[4] These two
motions (Subject and Object) have no existence apart from
each other. Thus there is no absolute existence in the physical
world ; all sensible existence is relative, or rather there
is no existence (εἶναι), *i.e.* nothing permanent, there is only
change (γίγνεσθαι), and this is always relative.[5] These objects

---

[1] *Metaph.* 986 b 32 *sqq.*

[2] The passages in which this view
is developed are *Theaet.* c. x. pp.
153 D-154 B ; c. xiii. pp. 156 A-157 B ;
c. xiv. pp. 159 C-160 C ; c. xxviii.

pp. 181 B-182 E.

[3] *Theaet.* pp. 153 E-154 A.

[4] Pp. 156 E-157 A.

[5] Pp. 156 E-157 A. Cp. p. 160 A-C.

of sense, αἰσθητά, are qualities (ποιότητες),[1] and what we call things, *e.g.* a man and a stone, are merely groups or bundles (ἀθροίσματα),[2] of these qualities. But these products, αἰσθητά, or qualities (including, of course, both individual qualities and those groups of qualities we call things) and sensations, αἰσθήσεις, have (as we have seen) no existence in themselves, but are constantly changing with the change of the Producers, for when the object meets with a different subject or the subject with a different object, the product is different ; thus no two sensations can be alike, and no two objects of sensation are alike.[3] As Hamilton said, no two men ever saw the same sun. Thus neither object nor subject, since they are constantly changing, can be said to be the same. Thus, so far as sensation goes (on the subjective side), personal identity is lost ; I am, not one and the same man throughout life, but a series of distinct men ; [4] and (on the objective side) since each quality is changing and is never the same, things (men, stones, etc.), being but bundles of these qualities, are ever changing and have no permanent existence. The products (τὰ γεννώμενα), both the qualities,[5] αἰσθητά, and the sensations, αἰσθήσεις,[6] are in flux. Thus, since the Products vary with different subjects and objects, the sensations of different men not only may, but must be, different ; a man's sensations are peculiar (ἴδια) to himself.[7] It is on this ground that Plato identifies the theory that knowledge is sensation with the Protagorean doctrine that man is the measure of all things—what seems to him is to him.[8]

The resemblance between this dynamical theory of sensation and certain recent speculations is curious. Herbert Spencer says : [9] " Literally, then, the so-called secondary attributes [of which especially Plato has been describing the origin] are neither objective nor subjective, but are the triple products of the subject, the object, and the environing activities. Sound, colour, heat, odour, and taste can be called attributes of body only in the sense that they imply in

---

[1] P. 182 A.
[2] P. 157 B.
[3] Pp. 159 A-160.
[4] P. 166 B.
[5] P. 182 C, D.

[6] P. 182 D, E.
[7] P. 154 A.
[8] Pp. 151 E-152 A.
[9] *Principles of Psychology*, vol. ii. p. 145, new ed.

body certain powers of reaction, which appropriate external actions call forth. These powers of reaction, however, are neither the attributes made known to us as sensations, nor those vibrations or undulations or molecular repulsions in which, as objectively considered, these attributes are commonly said to consist ; but they are the occult properties in virtue of which body modifies the forces brought to bear upon it. Nevertheless, it remains true that these attributes, as manifested to us, are dynamical, and in so far as the immediate relation is concerned, it remains true that in respect of these attributes the object is active and the subject is passive." Cp. Mill's *Logic* :[1] " Even those attributes of an object which might seem with greatest propriety to be called states of the object itself, its sensible qualities, its colour, hardness, shape, and the like, are in reality phenomena of causation, in which the substance is distinctly the agent, or producing cause, the patient being our own organs, and those of other sentient beings ". We may notice, too, the fullness of the nomenclature,[2] which seems to supply the deficiency complained of by Mill.[3]

The conclusion of the *Theaetetus* is thus negative ; what knowledge may be has not yet been discovered. One thing at least is certain that in the senses we look in vain for knowledge. This is expressed even more definitely in the conclusion of the *Cratylus*.[4] If in the sensible world all things are in flux ; in the first place, nothing in it has any existence, for before it can be said to be anything, it has slipped away[5] into something else : in the second place, nothing sensible can be known ; while we are in the very act of trying to know something sensible, it has altered. In short, neither knowing subject nor object known can have any existence, for existence implies permanence, but in the sensible world permanence is not.

---

[1] Vol. i. p. 387 (ed. 9).

[2] τὸ ποιοῦν—τὸ πάσχον, αἰσθητόν—αἴσθησις.

[3] *Exam. of Hamilton*, p. 215.

[4] Pp. 439 D-440 B.

[5] ἀεὶ ὑπεξέρχεται, *Crat.* p. 439 D.

IV

Having thus rejected the claims of sensation to knowledge, Plato proceeds in other works to unfold his own theory of knowledge and existence—the Ideal theory. That theory is first (I believe) definitely stated, though in different aspects, in the *Meno* and *Cratylus*. The notice of it in the *Meno* is but passing ; but the *Cratylus* is an important contribution to the subject, and as the latter dialogue is in some respects akin to the *Theaetetus*, it will be convenient to examine it next. In both the *Cratylus* and *Meno* the theory seems, from the terms in which it is spoken of, to be a novelty. The remark of Meno after the proof of immortality, and the reply of Socrates, seem to me to breathe something of the complacency which a thinker might feel at the moment of hitting upon so brilliant a theory as that of the Ideas.[1] And in the *Cratylus* the Ideal theory is spoken of as a dream,[2] and Plato does not insist upon it, or deny that the contrary theory (that of universal flux) may be right. In later life, the Ideas were for him the waking realities, the sensible world but a dream.[3] This contrast points decidedly to the early date of the *Cratylus*.

Different views may be taken of the scope and purpose of the *Cratylus*, but as my object is not to criticize the opinions of others, it will be enough to state my own. The *Cratylus*, it seems to me, is like the *Theaetetus*, a search after knowledge. Plato has tried to reach knowledge by way of sensation, but failing in that he tries another road, by way of words. He attempts to discover whether it may not be possible to acquire a knowledge of things by investigating the words which are their signs. It is true that both in the *Theaetetus* and *Cratylus* we detect an already formed conviction underlying the whole investigation that after all neither sensation nor words can furnish us with knowledge ; but nevertheless, the dialogues do really discuss the possibility of knowledge being gained by sensation and words.

---

[1] MEN. Εὖ μοι δοκεῖς λέγειν, ὦ Σώκρατες, οὐκ οἶδ' ὅπως. ΣΩ. Καὶ γὰρ ἐγὼ ἐμοί, ὦ Μένων, *Men.* p. 86 B.

[2] *Crat.* p. 439 C.

[3] *Tim.* p. 52 B, C ; *Rep.* p. 476 C, D ; cp. *ib.* pp. 520 C, 533 C, 534 C.

This view of the scope of the *Cratylus* is strongly confirmed by the conclusion of the dialogue, and it gives unity and consistency to the whole. This may be best seen by a survey of the dialogue. The *Cratylus* is divided into two main parts ; the first is the conversation of Socrates with Hermogenes, the second that of Socrates with Cratylus. Hermogenes holds that the connexion between things and their names is merely conventional and arbitrary,[1] Cratylus that the connexion is a natural necessity, that words have a natural application to the things they stand for.[2] The result of Socrates' conversation with Hermogenes is that (contrary to Hermogenes' original view) words are found to have a natural connexion with things, a connexion of resemblance or imitation ; or rather words *ought* to have (and if they are rightly formed *will* have) this resemblance to the things of which they are the names. For it is the function of a word to signify that of which it is the name, and this it can in itself only do by resembling or imitating the thing.[3] This, then, is the conclusion come to in the first part of the dialogue —names ought to be copies or likenesses of the things named.

The result of the second part of the dialogue is that (contrary to the original view of Cratylus) though words ought to be copies of things, yet, as a matter of fact, these copies may be quite mistaken ; they may, owing to a blunder of the name-giver (similar to the blunder of one who mistakes a portrait), have been applied to things which they do not all resemble. Now Cratylus had held that the only way of acquiring knowledge of things was by studying their names ; since names resemble things (he thought), we can gain a knowledge of things by studying the names which resemble them.[4] But Socrates has shown that though words *ought* to resemble things, they may fail to do so, and therefore one who trusted to names as his guides to knowledge would inevitably go astray. The conclusion of the dialogue is, that for a knowledge of things we must look to the things themselves, to their essences, not to their names. Now the things themselves, the essences of things, were, according to Plato, their ideas ; hence the dialogue closes with a sketch of the

[1] P. 384 D.
[2] P. 383 A, B.
[3] c. 34.
[4] P. 435 D, E.

Ideal theory, on the supposition of which alone (it is implied) is knowledge possible.

This outline may help to confirm the view that the aim of the dialogue is to show that knowledge is not to be gained by an examination of words. But for our purpose it is needful to go into greater detail. At an early stage of his conversation with Socrates, Hermogenes is represented as discarding, after a very brief argument, the theory which gave rise to so long and elaborate a discussion in the *Theaetetus*, the theory, namely, of Protagoras, that man is the measure of all things, that things are to a man as they seem to him.[1] He also rejects the doctrine of Euthydemus that all things always stand in the same relation to everybody.[2] It remains that there must be some things which have an absolute existence, which are not relative to us, but are wholly independent of, do not change with, our perceptions of them ; such things have their relations wholly confined to themselves, they are absolute.[3] Here we have got beyond the position of the *Theaetetus* ; there we saw nothing but the changing elements of the sensible world, elements which (it was found) could only exist in relation to each other ; they were, moreover, in constant change, so that they could not be said truly to be, only to become. This admission, therefore, of an absolute existence[4] is highly important for the Platonic development.

Socrates proceeds to include actions amongst those absolute existences, on the ground that our actions must conform to natural laws ; we cannot conform nature to our actions. Our actions are thus in themselves (not necessarily in their origin) absolute, *i.e.* not dependent on our wishes. Now naming is an action ; it must therefore, like all other actions, be subject to natural laws ; names must be naturally adapted to things, they cannot be arbitrarily applied by us.[5] In order to discover the natural application of

---

[1] c. iv. pp. 385 E-386 D.

[2] P. 386 D.

[3] οὐκοῦν εἰ μήτε πᾶσι πάντα ἐστὶν ὁμοίως ἅμα καὶ ἀεὶ μήτε ἑκάστῳ ἰδίᾳ ἕκαστον τῶν ὄντων ἐστί, δῆλον δή, ὅτι αὐτὰ αὑτῶν οὐσίαν ἔχοντά τινα βεβαιόν ἐστι τὰ πράγματα, οὐ πρὸς ἡμᾶς οὐδὲ ὑφ' ἡμῶν, ἑλκόμενα ἄνω καὶ κάτω τῷ ἡμετέρῳ φαντάσματι, ἀλλὰ καθ' αὑτὰ πρὸς τὴν αὑτῶν οὐσίαν ἔχοντα ᾗπερ πέφυκε, p. 386, D, E.

[4] τὰ ὄντα, p. 387 E.

[5] P. 387.

names to things, a number of words are analysed. These are found to be compounded of shorter words. The compound words derive their meaning from, are significant by reason of, the shorter words.[1]

But to explain the significance of words by analysing them into shorter significant words is only to throw the question a step further back, for we at once ask, whence do these shorter words derive their significance? This regress process cannot be infinite; we must at last come back to certain primary names from which all other names are derived. Indeed we seem to have hit upon some of this class, *e.g.* τὸ ἰόν, τὸ ῥέον, τὸ δοῦν, for we found that a very large number of words could be analysed into these. The question then is : whence do these primary words drive their significance? The answer is, by imitating the things of which they are names. But words are not mere imitations of the sounds of things (for then certain musical airs, vocal imitations of beasts, etc., would be words), nor of the shapes and colours of things (for these are imitated by painting) ; words must be imitations not of the sounds, shapes, and colours, but of the essence of things.

[This passage is to be marked. The essences of things which names are to imitate are, of course, the Ideas, and these Ideas are here shown to be quite distinct from the sensible qualities of things.] The analysis is then carried to its last stage by analysing these apparently primary words into their letters, and by showing that these letters have a natural significance ; ρ naturally signifies motion, for in uttering it the tongue vibrates ; therefore it was used in the formation of words signifying motion, ῥεῖν, τρόμος, etc.[2] Again, because of the compression of the tongue which takes place in pronouncing δ and τ, the namer used these letters to imitate binding (δεσμός) and standing (στάσις). So other letters have a natural resemblance to certain things and are therefore used to form the names which denote these things. At this stage, where it has been found that the

---

[1] *E.g.* Ποσειδῶν is said to be compounded of ποσί and δεσμόν or of πόλλ' εἰδώς or of ὁ σείων ; Δημήτηρ is διδοῦσα μήτηρ ; φρόνησις = φορᾶς καὶ

ῥοῦ νόησις ; ἀνδρεία = ἡ ἐναντία ῥοή, δειλία = δ δεῖ λίαν ; τὸ λυσιτελοῦν = τὸ τῆς φορᾶς λύον τὸ τέλος, etc.

[2] P. 426 A-E.

correctness of a word consists in its being so formed out of letters and syllables as that it shall resemble or be a copy of the essence of the thing named, the first part of the dialogue (the conversation of Socrates with Hermogenes) comes to an end.[1]

In the conversation with Cratylus which follows, Socrates forces Cratylus (very much against his will) to admit that words (like all other copies) may misrepresent their originals. Moreover, Socrates points out that some names are significant by convention only. The Eretrians, he says, pronounce σκληρότηρ where the Athenians say σκληρότης; thus the same meaning is conveyed to the Athenians and Eretrians by the different letters ρ and σ. Further, λ in σκληρότης was seen to be the natural letter to express smoothness; yet here it appears in a word expressing roughness. Yet none the less do we understand the meaning of σκληρότης or σκληρότηρ; these words are significant, it appears, not because of the letters which compose them (for λ signifies naturally the reverse of roughness, and ρ and σ are different, yet convey the same meaning), but because custom has made the signification familiar : but custom is convention. We have thus to admit that custom and convention contribute to the signification of names.[2] The conclusion of the discussion on the correctness of names is that names ought, as far as possible, to resemble the things which they represent, and the more they are composed of letters and syllables which do resemble the thing, the better they are ; but this principle cannot be carried out completely, we must admit an element of convention.[3]

The result thus reached is sufficient to disprove the theory of knowledge held by Cratylus. Cratylus thinks that not only the best but the only way of acquiring a knowledge of things is to study their names ; for since the names resemble the things, by studying the names we gain a

[1] P. 427 D.
[2] P. 435 B.
[3] c. 41, p. 435 C ἐμοὶ μὲν οὖν καὶ αὐτῷ ἀρέσκει μὲν κατὰ τὸ δυνατὸν ὅμοια εἶναι τὰ ὀνόματα τοῖς πράγμασιν· ἀλλὰ μὴ ὡς ἀληθῶς τὸ τοῦ Ἑρμογένους, γλίσχρα ᾖ ἡ ὁλκὴ αὕτη τῆς ὁμοιότητος,

ἀναγκαῖον δὲ ᾖ καὶ τῷ φορτικῷ τούτῳ προσχρῆσθαι, τῇ ξυνθήκῃ, εἰς ὀνομάτων ὀρθότητα. ἐπεὶ ἴσως κατά γε τὸ δυνατὸν κάλλιστ᾽ ἂν λέγοιτο, ὅταν ἢ πᾶσιν ἢ ὡς πλείστοις ὁμοίοις λέγηται, τοῦτο δ᾽ ἐστὶ προσῆκουσιν, αἴσχιστα δὲ τοὐναντίον.

knowledge of the things which they resemble.[1] This is of course disproved by the conclusion come to above, that names, though they ought to represent, may actually mis-represent things ; the name-giver (who is supposed to be the original Law-giver) may have made mistakes in applying names to things, the names may not really have resembled the things which he believed them to resemble. Thus a study of names might lead to error instead of to knowledge. Moreover, the theory leads to an impossibility. For Cratylus admits that the original Name-givers knew the things to which they gave names. But if the only way to know things is through their names, how could these Name-givers know things before they had given them names ? Thus, in order to gain a knowledge of things or realities [2] we must look to something else than their names ; it must be possible to know things without the help of names. Surely the only way of acquiring a knowledge of things is to study the things themselves both separately and in their mutual relations, if they are akin.[3] The study of names may indeed disclose to us the views which the first Name-givers held with regard to the nature of things, but these views may have been mistaken, and we must not allow ourselves to be deceived by them. From the numerous words which we have dis-covered on analysis to be significant of motion, it would appear that the original Name-givers held the Heraclitean doctrine of the flux of all things : but what of that ? It is just as likely that these Name-givers grew giddy from looking about to examine things, and so fancied that all things were whirling about, as that all things are really in motion.[4] I often dream, says Socrates, of a state of things very different from that of a universal flux. The particulars of sense are fleeting ; beautiful faces come and go, and so with all beautiful things ; but apart from beautiful things there is Beauty itself ; apart from good things there is Goodness itself. These are not transitory, they exist and do not pass away. In the world of sense there is neither existence nor knowledge : that cannot be which is always changing ; and that which is always changing cannot be

[1] Pp. 435 E-436 A.
[2] τὰ ὄντα, p. 438 E.
[3] P. 438 E.
[4] P. 411 B, C ; *cf.* 439 C and 440 C, D.

known, for before we have apprehended it, it is altered. If motion, then, be universal, there can be no existence, no true being either of subject or of object, either of knower or of known. But if there be after all a knower and a known, if there be Beauty, Goodness, and all such realities (ἐν ἕκαστον τῶν ὄντων), then are these existences exempt from the stream of change? Whether this or the Heraclitean be the true doctrine it is not easy to decide. At all events no sensible man should risk his soul by trusting in words and the men who made them, presuming that he knows by their means that there is nothing stable in himself or in things, but that everything is flowing away like pots on a river.[1]

Such is an outline of the dialogue, sufficient perhaps for the purpose in hand. It may help to show that the thought underlying the whole dialogue is knowledge, and knowledge of certain permanent, unchanging entities, the Platonic Ideas. Names ought to represent the essence (οὐσία) of things, and this essence is something quite apart from the physical qualities of things, their colour, shape, sound, etc.[2] These essences which loom dimly in the background of the *Cratylus*, and of which we catch a somewhat clearer glimpse only at the close of the dialogue, are soon to burst on us in more than rainbow brightness in the *Phaedrus* and *Republic*. The point to remember here is that these essences are distinct from the physical qualities of things.[3] The technical words for these essences were of course εἶδος and ἰδέα, and the first passage in Plato where the former may be thought to be used in this special sense is *Cratylus*, p. 389 B.[4] It is true that the words εἶδος and ἰδέα occur in a sense somewhat similar to the later Platonic usage in a passage in *Euthyphro*.[5] But the words are used in the *Euthyphro* in a merely logical sense to denote general notions, not (as in later dialogues) in a metaphysical sense, to denote general existences. The

---

[1] P. 440 C.

[2] c. 34.

[3] *Crat.* c. 34.

[4] ΣΩ. ποῖ βλέπων ὁ τέκτων τὴν κερ-κίδα ποιεῖ; ἆρ' οὐ πρὸς τοιοῦτόν τι ὃ πέφυκε κερκίζειν; ΕΡΜ. Πάνυ γε. ΣΩ. Τί δέ; ἂν καταγῇ αὐτῷ ἡ κερκὶς ποι-οῦντι, πότερον πάλιν ποιήσει ἄλλην πρὸς

τὴν κατεαγυῖαν βλέπων; ἢ πρὸς ἐκεῖνο τὸ εἶδος, πρὸς ὅπερ καὶ ἣν κατέαξεν ἐποίει; ΕΡΜ. πρὸς ἐκεῖνο, ἔμοιγε δοκεῖ. ΣΩ. Οὐκοῦν ἐκεῖνο δικαιότατ' ἂν αὐτὸ ὃ ἔστι κερκὶς καλέσαιμεν; ΕΡΜ. Ἔμοιγε δοκεῖ.

[5] P. 6 D, E (quoted above, p. 13).

question whether the εἶδος (that of the κερκίς or weaving-rod), alluded to in *Cratylus*, p. 389 B, is or is not a genuine Platonic Idea, is of some importance for the development of the Platonic doctrine. For if the *Cratylus* be, as I take it to be, one of the earliest dialogues in which the doctrine of Ideas appears, and if this εἶδος of p. 389 B be a true Platonic Idea, then we must admit that from the outset Plato recognized ideas of *things*, and not only of things in general, but of artificial things. That he did at least later recognize ideas of things and of artificial things we know from Plato himself. But Plato acknowledges [1] that he often hesitated whether to make ideas of things or not. I am inclined to believe that at the outset he did not suppose ideas of sensible things (*i.e.* substances, trees, houses, men, etc.) at all ; and if this be so, the εἶδος of the weaving-rod in *Cratylus*, p. 389 B, must be explained otherwise than by supposing it to be a pure idea. The explanation seems simple enough ; a carpenter when about to manufacture any article first forms a picture of it in his mind ; and this mental picture he uses as a model. It is this mental picture of which Plato is here speaking and which he designates by the word εἶδος, a natural word to employ since it means properly "visible appearance". And even when he did undoubtedly come to use the word in a technical sense to denote a peculiar invention of his own system, he naturally did not always accurately distinguish between the popular and the technical sense ; the two must have run into each other to some extent in his mind. Still it may be urged that just after speaking of the εἶδος of the weaving-rod, he goes on to speak of the εἶδος of a name in a way which leaves no doubt that he has in view the true Idea of a name ; and that if the εἶδος of a name is an Idea, so must be the εἶδος of the weaving-rod.[2] In face of this I do not insist upon the explanation of the εἶδος of the weaving-rod given above, but only maintain that at first Plato, if he made ideas of things, at least had not them primarily in view ; that the notions which he primarily idealized and which he regarded as of paramount importance were not concrete notions of things,

[1] *Parmen.* p. 130 B, C.
[2] *Cf.* p. 389 D αὐτὸ ἐκεῖνο ὃ ἔστιν ὄνομα, p. 390 A τὸ τοῦ ὀνόματος εἶδος, and immediately below τὸ προσῆκον εἶδος κερκίδος.

but abstract notions of qualities, etc., and especially those
abstract notions on which Socrates and Plato himself in his
more purely Socratic days had dwelt—moral notions. Con-
sistently with this, when the Ideal theory makes (at the close
of the *Cratylus*) its first appearance in its normal shape, the
notions idealized are those of Beauty and Goodness ; these
are classed among realities (τὰ ὄντα).[1]

Thus there is in the *Cratylus* a distinct advance on the
Theaetetus. The *Theaetetus* left us floating on the river of
sense : neither existence nor knowledge had yet raised their
heads above the tossing flood, or if knowledge had appeared,
it was but a faint and partial glimpse we had of it.[2] In the
Cratylus there is at least a strong hope held out of a *terra
firma* ; the voice of the restless waters is still heard [3] but it
is farther off, they are retiring and leaving the solid ground,
or what Plato took for such. The land seems (so far as we
can descry it) to be composed of general notions. In *Cratylus* [4]
there is a noteworthy passage. It is suggested that as all
words may be analysed into their letters, so perhaps all things
may be reducible to a certain number of elements, which
may explain the existence of all-derived things.[5] These ele-
mentary existences are no doubt the Platonic Ideas. The
multitude of particular things is reduced to unity by being
classified ; their infinity (if I may say so) becomes finite. It
was no doubt in class notions that Plato sought these ele-
mentary existences (of which he here speaks) which were to
explain the existence of all else. Thus Plato seems to have
made Ideas, not of every particular thing, but only of classes,
of universals, not of particulars. It has been suggested, I
believe, that the *Cratylus* was written for the express purpose
of thus limiting the sphere of the Ideal world by showing that
Ideas were only of general notions. But this seems to me
unduly to limit the scope of the dialogue. However, the
result of the *Cratylus* is this : that it is at least possible that
general notions (goodness, beauty, etc.) have a permanent

---

[1] P. 439 C.

[2] *Theaet.* pp. 184 B-187 B.

[3] *Crat.* cc. 18-33, pp. 401 B-421 C
and pp. 439 D-440 D.

[4] P. 424 D.

[5] The passage is unfortunately
corrupt, but the general sense seems
plain. Stallbaum's correction (far too
violent to be admissible) seems to give
the sense rightly τὰ ὄντα ἐπισκέψασθαι
for ὀνόματα ἐπιθεῖναι.

existence, exempt from the flux of the sensible world, and that these permanent existences can alone be known.

V

The *Meno* is like the *Cratylus*, one of the earliest, perhaps the very earliest, dialogue in which we find a distinct statement of the Ideal theory. But the aspect in which that doctrine appears in the *Meno* is quite different from that presented in the *Cratylus*. In the *Meno* the Ideal doctrine is used to prove the immortality of the soul by means of the peculiarly Platonic notion of ἀνάμνησις or recollection. The doctrine reappears in the *Phaedo* and *Phaedrus*, but in none of the other dialogues of Plato (with the exception perhaps of a faint allusion in the *Timaeus*, which I shall point out in its place). This, then, is a common feature of the *Meno*, *Phaedrus*, and *Phaedo*, and accordingly in an account of the Platonic Ideas, these dialogues may be conveniently taken together. Moreover, it is probable that they were written about the same time, the *Meno*, however, somewhat before the other two. For the *Meno*, as a whole, is essentially Socratic in its subject (the teachability of virtue) and in its negative results, as well as in minor peculiarities, *e.g.* the profession of ignorance,[1] the inability of Meno at first to grasp a general notion.[2] On the other hand, there are points in it which are characteristic of Plato himself, *e.g.* the immortality of the soul [3] and the closely allied doctrine of ἀνάμνησις,[4] and the distinction between knowledge and opinion.[5] The parody of the Empedoclean theory of sensation [6] is more Platonic than Socratic. This combination of Socratic and Platonic characteristics seems to indicate that the *Meno* is one of the early dialogues of the second period written at a time when Plato, while still preserving to some extent the Socratic mode of thought, had already conceived some of those doctrines which were peculiar to himself. The style of the language, too, is smooth and flowing ; it has the simplicity of the Socratic period without

[1] P. 71.
[2] Pp. 71 E *sqq.*
[3] Pp. 81 A *sqq.*
[4] Pp. 82 A *sqq.*
[5] P. 97.
[6] P. 76 D.

attaining to that brilliancy of diction which marks (*e.g.*) the *Phaedo* and *Symposium*. There is an allusion [1] to Ismenias the Theban which might be of use for determining the date, but the commentators are divided as to the year in which the transaction alluded to took place. On the whole, the probability is that the *Meno* was written between 390 and 380, probably nearer the former than the latter. The *Phaedrus* seems to have been written about the same time. From the way in which Lysias is spoken of in this dialogue, it cannot well have been written after 378 B.C., the date of Lysias's death. The tradition (recorded by Diogenes Laertius) that the *Phaedrus* was the earliest of the Platonic compositions is utterly disproved by internal evidence, and deserves no serious attention. The *Phaedrus* is an essentially Platonic, not Socratic dialogue. It may be safely ranked amongst the earlier compositions of that second period in which Plato gave to the Socratic theory of conceptual knowledge that peculiar development which is associated with his name. Thus the *Phaedrus* was probably written some little time before 380. The *Symposium*, which is connected in style and matter with the *Phaedrus*, was not written before 385 (for by an anachronism it contains [2] an allusion to the destruction of Mantinea by the Lacedaemonians, which took place in that year), and probably not after 370, when Mantinea was rebuilt. The *Symposium* seems to be later than the *Phaedrus*; as a dramatic work it is far more brilliant than the latter. While the *Phaedrus* is marked by a more youthful freshness and enthusiasm, reminding one of the freshness of spring, the *Symposium* has all the mellow richness of a glorious autumn, πάντ᾽ ὦσδεν θέρεος μάλα πίονος, ὦσδε δ᾽ ὀπώρας.[3] This inference is confirmed by an apparent allusion in the *Symposium* [4] to the *Phaedrus*. (This reference, as well as some other facts which help to determine the dates of the *Phaedrus*, *Symposium*, and *Republic*, I have borrowed from my notes of Mr. Jackson's lectures on the *Phaedrus*.) The *Phaedo* is now generally admitted to have preceded the *Republic*, and probably to have followed the *Symposium*. But the *Republic* seems

[1] P. 90 A.   [3] Theocr. vii. 143.
[2] P. 193 A.   [4] P. 182 A.

from internal evidence to have been composed between 382
and 371. On the whole, then, we are justified in regarding
the *Meno, Phaedrus, Symposium,* and *Phaedo* as a group
of dialogues which followed each other at not very long
intervals, in the order in which I have named them.
In the *Meno* the Ideal theory appears in connexion
with the Platonic doctrines of ἀνάμνησις and (founded on it)
immortality. It is true that in the earlier works [1] the notion
of immortality is alluded to, but only in a popular and
(in the *Apology*) hesitating way ; it is not laid down as a
doctrine which we have philosophical grounds for believing
in. Again, in the *Gorgias* (which ranks among the earlier
compositions of the second period, but whether it is later or
earlier than the *Meno* it is difficult to decide), the doctrine
is treated in a mythical and popular way, but nevertheless
with a degree of distinctness and confidence,[2] which does
not appear in the *Apology* and *Crito.* The definition, too,
of death in the *Gorgias* [3] is exactly that of the *Phaedo.*[4]
Still, though these and many other circumstances show that
the *Gorgias* was composed not very long before the *Phaedo*,
the former does not contain a philosophical account either
of the Ideal theory or of immortality, and may therefore for
the present purpose be left out of account.

The passage in the *Meno* which is of importance for
the present subject is found cc. 14-21, pp. 80 D-86 C. It is
introduced by a doubt raised by Meno as to the possibility
of seeking for what we do not know.[5] This was an eristic
quibble of the day, intended to demonstrate the impossibility
of learning anything ; Socrates undertakes to show the
possibility of learning. He first of all appeals to Pindar
and the poets who maintain that the soul, while it goes
through the processes of life and death, yet never perishes ;
thus being immortal, and having been often born, it has
seen and learned all things. Thus after being born once
more into life, it may in time by recollection recover the
knowledge of virtue and other things which it previously
possessed ; the recollection of one thing will help to call up

---

[1] *Apol.* c. 32, pp. 40 C-41 C ; *Crito,*
c. 16, p. 54 B, C.
[2] Cp. *Gorg.* pp. 523 A, 524 A, 526 D.
[3] P. 524 B.
[4] P. 64 C.
[5] P. 80 E.

a whole train of other recollections   All that we call learning thus consists in recollecting that which we knew before birth.[1] To prove this position, Socrates cross-examines a slave of Meno. This slave has never been taught mathematics, but in answer to a series of leading questions propounded by Socrates, he evolves a mathematical theorem, viz. that a square, to be double the area of another square, must be described on the diagonal (or on a line equal to the diagonal) of that square.   At first the slave thinks the side of the new square must be made double the length of the side of the old square, if the new square is to be double the area of the original square ; [2] afterwards, seeing his mistake, he admits his ignorance ; [3] afterwards he is led to the proper conclusion that the square described on the *diagonal* of a square is double the area of the latter square.[4] The slave thus exhibits a knowledge of geometry, and has never learned it in this life ; the inference is that he acquired the knowledge in that antenatal state when he was not yet a man.   Thus both when he was not a man and when he is, he is shown to have a knowledge of geometry : but the time during which he was not a man, and that during which he was and is so, together make up all time.   Therefore for all time, *i.e.* for eternity, his soul has had knowledge, and has thus been immortal.

Thus in the *Meno* the Ideal doctrine has advanced a step.   The doctrine is regarded subjectively as a theory of knowing, nothing is told us of the objects thus known, *i.e.* the Ideas.   This point of view is the opposite to that of the *Cratylus* ; in the latter dialogue the light (such as it is) is thrown on the objects of knowledge, while the knowing subject is left in shadow ; the objects are declared to be formless, colourless, soundless, essences of which names should be the copies, the self-good, self-beautiful, etc., which are unchanging, exalted above the flux of the sensible world.   In the *Meno* all that we are told is that the soul has acquired knowledge in an antenatal state which it can revive by recollection in the present life.   Taken thus by themselves, the doctrines of the *Cratylus* and *Meno* seem

[1] P. 81 D.   [3] P. 84 E.
[2] P. 82 E.   [4] P. 85 B.

quite distinct, and were it not for other dialogues, we would hardly have suspected that they were two different sides of the same theory. We shall presently find that the two aspects, the subjective and objective, which are separately presented in the *Meno* and *Cratylus* respectively, are united in the *Phaedrus*, which contains an account both of the objects of knowledge (the Ideas) and of the subjective process of recollection. The latter dialogue, along with the *Phaedo*, shows us that in the *Meno* an important addition has been made to the representation of the Ideal theory given or hinted at in the *Cratylus*. The *Meno*, however, gives us some information which is not to be found in the *Phaedrus*. From the *Meno* it would appear that this " recollection " gave us not so much detached facts as connected pieces of reasoning (exemplified by the mathematical theorem described above), whereas in the *Phaedrus* the knowledge it imparts seems to be mostly of separate, unconnected Ideas : in other words, the knowledge supplied by " recollection " is in the *Phaedrus* intuitive, in the *Meno* discursive. Further, it is to be noted that the notions given by recollection in the *Meno* are mathematical. We should notice, however, p. 81 C, where of the notions given by recollection only that of virtue is specified. This is seen to be of some importance when we recollect the subject of the *Meno*. We ought not indeed to regard the passage on ἀνάμνησις as unconnected with the rest of the dialogue; it ought not to be taken out of its setting. The object of the *Meno* is to discover whether virtue is teachable ; but before this can be decided, the preliminary question, what is virtue ? must be answered. After all attempts to define it have proved futile, this passage about ἀνάμνησις occurs, in which Plato intends to hint that a knowledge of virtue can only be acquired by a recollection of the Idea of virtue. Hence the allusion to ἀρετή.[1]

VI

The subject of the *Phaedrus* is doubtless rhetoric ; on no other view can the dialogue be regarded as a consistent unity. But the second speech of Socrates [2] contains im-

[1] P. 81 C.   [2] From pp. 243 E to 257 B.

portant matter for the Ideal theory. The substance of it (leaving out unnecessary mythical details) is as follows. Human souls are immortal. (The proof of immortality [1] does not rest upon ἀνάμνησις as in the *Meno* and *Phaedo*, but upon the existence of motion.) The soul consists of three parts : first the rational, second the passionate or spirited, third the appetitive. The reason is the proper governor of the soul ; the appetitive part is ill-disposed, full of low desires, and it rebels against the reason. The emotional (or passionate) part aids the reason in its struggle against appetite, but both the emotional and appetitive parts are subordinate to the reason, like horses to the charioteer. The natural home for souls is the upper world where dwell the gods. In the heavenly regions the gods and human souls which accompany them behold at stated periods the world of reality. The real [2] consists of colourless, shapeless, and formless essences which can be apprehended by reason alone. Particular portions of this real world are pure justice, pure temperance, pure knowledge.[3] It is this real world which is the object of true knowledge,[4] and this true knowledge is the food of the soul; when deprived of this its proper food, the soul has to feed on mere opinion.[5] So long as a soul is able to obtain a sight of this world of reality, it remains in the upper region with the gods ; but when the reason, hampered by the lower parts of the soul,[6] is no longer able to view the world of realities, it grows forgetful and sinks down to earth, and so assumes a human shape.[7] All men have at some time or other beheld the real world, for no soul that has not done so can take upon it a human body.[8] If a man lives a philosophical life he may in time (after three such lives) return to the upper world ; if he lives a bad life, his soul at death is degraded by passing into lower and lower forms. Few souls remember much of the realities of the other world ; most, on entering on this life, become polluted with sin, and so forget what they had seen before. Of the realities or Ideas only Beauty has a

---

[1] Pp. 245 C-246 A.

[2] τὸ ὄν, p. 247 D.

[3] P. 247 D.

[4] περὶ ἣν [*scil.* τὴν ἀχρώματον κτλ. οὐσίαν] τὸ τῆς ἀληθοῦς ἐπιστήμης γένος.

[5] P. 248 B.

[6] P. 248 A.

[7] P. 248 C; cp. p. 246 C.

[8] P. 249 C.

sensible likeness.   The others (justice, temperance, etc.) have
no visible copies here on earth.   Accordingly, it is the recollection of the Idea of Beauty that is most easily awakened.
When a man sees, *e.g.* a beautiful face, he (if he be of a philo-
sophic soul) is reminded of the Idea of Beauty, and this
recollection wakes a longing for the other world ; this longing gets its only satisfaction from the sight of the beautiful
form which awakened it.   Accordingly, he who is thus reminded desires to be constantly with the beautiful person
who forms the link between him and the world of Ideas.
This is true love.   If the lover and beloved live a pure life
of philosophical communion, they will at death have com-
pleted one of the three stages preparatory to a return to
their heavenly home.

Such is a bare outline of one of the loftiest and most
brilliant passages in Plato.   In it a great advance has been
made in distinctness and positiveness both on the objective
and subjective side of the Ideal theory.   The Ideas which
were dimly conceived in the *Cratylus* now stand out sharp
and clear, resplendent with a more than earthly light, lying
in a region above the vault of heaven,[1] and contemplated by
the gods and by human souls at their best.   How far, if at all,
this localization of the Ideas was serious, we cannot say; it
is not repeated in any other dialogue.   From the *Timaeus* [2]
we would certainly infer that the Ideas were not in space, and
this is confirmed by Aristotle, who asks [3] why Plato did not
suppose the Ideas to exist in space.   But even if Plato had
held throughout that the Ideas did not exist in space, this would
not necessarily have prevented him from placing them up in
the supra-celestial region, since that region may have been
supposed by him to be outside space, just as Aristotle himself
believed in a supra-celestial region which yet was neither in
space nor time and which contained many wonderful beings.[4]
Indeed the description of this upper region by Aristotle is
very similar to that of Plato in the *Phaedrus*, and the notion
would seem to have been borrowed from his master.

---

[1] Pp. 247 A-C τὰ ἔξω τοῦ οὐρανοῦ—τὸν
ὑπερουράνιον τόπον.

[2] P. 52 B.

[3] *Phys. Aus.* Δ p. 209 b 34 ; this
reference I take from Bonitz, *Ind.
Arist.* p. 599 b 2, 3.

[4] *De Caelo*, i. c. 8, p. 279.

We must note the Ideas themselves. There are specified Ideas of Justice, Temperance, Knowledge,[1] and of Justice, Temperance, and Beauty.[2] No ideas of material substances are hinted at. This evidence, though purely negative, favours so far the view I have expressed, that at first Plato did not make Ideas of things, of sensible substances at all. The Ideal theory seems primarily to have been intended as an explanation of the origin of those notions which are not immediately given by sense. We have (Plato may have reflected) notions of men, horses, tables, etc. ; whence do these notions come ? From the senses evidently. We have also notions of beauty, justice, knowledge, etc. ; whence do these come ? Not from sense—none of them are objects of sensation ; we can never, therefore, have acquired them from experience : but experience (*i.e.* sense experience) began with our birth ; therefore these notions of justice, etc., must have been in our minds previous to birth, our soul must therefore have existed before birth, and in that antenatal state it must have acquired those ideas which are not copies of sensible things. This view, that at the time when Plato wrote the *Phaedrus* he did not conceive ideas of sensible substances, is confirmed by the way in which he treats beauty. It alone of the Ideas has a visible counterpart.[3] Now this could hardly have been said if Plato had believed at the time he wrote the *Phaedrus* in Ideal horses, beds, etc., for these of course would have had visible counterparts on earth. Thus both from this positive statement and from the negative evidence (the want of any certain mention of the Idea of a sensible substance), the conclusion seems necessary that at first Plato did not conceive of Ideas of concrete, sensible substances. This is true of the *Meno*, the *Cratylus* (as I have tried to show), *Phaedrus*, and (as we shall see) of the *Phaedo*. The description of reality (οὐσία) as colourless, shapeless, and intangible[4] is not decisive on this point, for as we saw, in the *Cratylus* the essence even of material things is supposed to be something quite apart from their material qualities.[5]

[1] P. 247 D.
[2] P. 250 B.
[3] P. 250.

[4] *Phaedr.* p. 247 C.
[5] *Crat.* c. 34, p. 422.

This is but a part of a wider conclusion to which the perusal of these dialogues (of the *Phaedrus* especially) must lead us ; it is this, that the Ideal theory was started from an ontological, not from a logical, point of view, and that, accordingly, at first Plato did not, as he afterwards did, assume an Idea corresponding to every class-name.[1] That Plato in this early stage did not assume an Idea corresponding to every common notion which we have is shown, I think, conclusively by the fact that in the *Phaedrus* ideas are evidently assumed only of what is good. There is an Idea specified of Justice, but none of Injustice ; of Temperance, but not of Intemperance ; of Knowledge, but not of Ignorance ; of Beauty, but not of Ugliness. But injustice, intemperance, ignorance, and ugliness are as truly common notions as their respective contraries, and had the Ideal theory been intended to explain our common notions in general, Ideas of vices must have been assumed just as much as of virtues. That as a fact Plato did not assume ideas of injustice, etc., seems conclusively proved by such passages as *Phaedrus*, p. 250, where it is said that some souls on coming into the world betake themselves to injustice and so forget what they saw in the world of ideas. But had injustice been one of the Ideas, men by practising it on earth would have been reminded by it of the Ideas. The fact that injustice produces forgetfulness of the Ideal world surely shows that there was no Idea of Injustice to be remembered. Again in p. 248 C, to be tainted with evil (κακία) and to forget the Ideal world are represented as simultaneous. Had there been an idea of evil, to have become evil would have been a sure way of recollecting, not of forgetting, the Ideas. And the description given in p. 250 B, C of the objects in the Ideal world and of the state of the soul in contemplating them, is wholly inconsistent with the notion that there were Ideas of evil.[2] It is not, we must observe,

---

[1] *Rep.* x. p. 596 A εἶδος γάρ πού τι ἕν ἕκαστον εἰώθαμεν τίθεσθαι περὶ ἕκαστα τὰ πολλά, οἶς ταὐτὸν ὄνομα ἐπιφέρομεν. When he wrote this, the originally ontological theory was influenced by logical considerations.

[2] κάλλος δὲ τότ' ἦν ἰδεῖν λαμπρόν,

ὅτε σὺν εὐδαίμονι χορῷ μακαρίαν ὄψιν τε καὶ θέαν, ἑπόμενοι μετὰ μὲν Διὸς ἡμεῖς, ἄλλοι δὲ μετ' ἄλλου θεῶν, εἴδόν τε καὶ ἐτελοῦντο τῶν τελετῶν ἣν θέμις λέγειν μακαριωτάτην, ἣν ὠργιάζομεν ὀλόκληροι μὲν αὐτοὶ ὄντες καὶ ἀπαθεῖς κακῶν ὅσα ἡμᾶς ἐν ὑστέρῳ χρόνῳ ὑπ-

that in the case of pairs of contraries, Plato made an Idea of only one of the pair ; for where the contraries were not (like justice and injustice, courage and cowardice) opposed as good and evil, he had no hesitation in making ideas of both contraries, e.g. of greatness and smallness,[1] heat and cold.[2] But of qualities distinctly bad, Plato never really constructed Ideas. It is therefore idle for Zeller to say that there were Ideas of Evil and Vice [3] and to quote in support *Theaetetus*, p. 176 E (where the Ideal theory is not enunciated at all), and *Republic*, v. p. 476, for there Plato is not describing the Ideal world, but only distinguishing those who know from those who do not ; those who can rise to the general notions of justice and injustice, good and evil ; those who can form such general notions are, he says, philosophers, those who cannot are φιλοθεάμονες. Thus the passage has really reference to knowing, not to being ; and (for the sake of logical consistency) to twist it into an affirmation of an Idea of Vice is to run counter to the whole tendency of Plato's philosophy. In no one place does he speak of an αὐτὴ αἰσχρότης, αὐτὴ ἀδικία, etc., and say that things are κακά by partaking in the αὐτὴ κακία, that they are αἰσχρά by partaking in the αὐτὴ αἰσχρότης, and so on. And the fact that he does not do so is all the more striking, since in the *Phaedo*, immediately after insisting on an Ideal beauty by which all beautiful things are beautiful, he at once passes to a pair of contrary qualities (viz. great and small) and says that great things are great by partaking in greatness, small things small by partaking in smallness ; thus markedly passing over the Idea of a contrary quality, where that contrary is bad, though introducing immediately afterwards ideas of both members of a pair of contraries, where these contraries are indifferent.[4] We must conclude, then, against Zeller [5] (1) that originally Plato did not suppose " an Idea corresponding to every general concept without exception " ; and (2) that among the concepts so excluded from the Ideal world are to be numbered certainly

---

ἔμενεν, ὁλόκληρα δὲ καὶ ἁπλᾶ καὶ ἀτρεμῆ
καὶ εὐδαίμονα φάσματα μνούμενοί τε καὶ
ἐποπτεύοντες ἐν αὐγῇ καθαρᾷ, καθαροὶ
ὄντες καὶ ἀσήμαντοι τούτου ὃ νῦν σῶμα
περιφέροντες ὀνομάζομεν.

[1] *Phaedo*, p. 100 E.
[2] *Id.* p. 103 C.
[3] P. 273, Eng. tr.
[4] *Phaedo*, c. 49, p. 100 B-E.
[5] P. 273, note, and p. 274.

(*a*) the concepts of evil, without exception, and probably (*b*) all concepts of material substances. It cannot therefore be that Plato started the Ideal theory as a means of explaining all our general notions ; for Ideas were (we see) assumed originally of only certain classes of concepts. And of what classes of concepts in particular ? Just of those we should have expected, viz. the concepts with which Socrates most of his life, and Plato in his younger days, busied themselves, the concepts of Beauty,[1] Goodness,[2] Justice and Temperance,[3] and Knowledge.[4] Thus in the Ideas we recognize simply our old friends the Socratic general notions, only their old rags [5] are exchanged for garments of such wondrous beauty, that our dazzled eyes can scarcely recognize the likeness.

How possibly (to return to the attack) could Plato (in the *Republic*) have made the Idea of Good supreme above all the other ideas, if he had supposed an Idea of Evil, which must have ranked equally with that of the Good, just as the Idea of Greatness ranked with that of Smallness ? This elevation of the Idea of Good seems possible only on the supposition that he contemplated ideas only of good or of indifferent things ; that thus in the case of contraries he idealized both, only if they were in themselves indifferent, but that where one contrary was bad he made no Idea of it. He would get a couple of parallel lists, one of good qualities, etc. (justice, etc.), the other of bad qualities, etc. (injustice, etc.). Ideas were assumed only of the former. But the common feature of the former list is that each member of it is good ; goodness is thus that in which all the ideas resemble each other, it is the common feature of all the ideas ; it is therefore the Idea of Ideas. Thus the supremacy ascribed in the *Republic* to the Idea of Good admits of an explanation, while on the theory that there were Ideas of evil, it is inexplicable. Later in life Plato seems to have abandoned the Ideal theory (at least in the form in which it appears in the *Phaedrus*), and this was perhaps due to the fact that he saw [6] that logic compelled him to make an Idea of every common notion, and

---

[1] *Crat.* pp. 439 C, 440 B ; *Phaedr.* p. 250 B.
[2] *Crat. ll.cc.*
[3] *Phaedr.* pp. 247 D, 250 B.

[4] *Phaedr.* p. 247 D, E.
[5] Cp. Xen. *Mem.* i. 2. 37.
[6] *Rep.* x. p. 596 A.

hence of bad things as much as of good. This may have
led him to the adoption of metaphysical principles according
to which Good and Evil did not thus stand over against each
other as co-ordinate. Such principles are the πέρας and
ἄπειρον, which are not co-ordinate ; ἄπειρον (representing
evil) is subordinate to πέρας (representing good).

Before quitting the *Phaedrus* we should observe the law
of the human understanding.[1] The method of understanding
(it is said) is to pass from a number of sensations to a unity
collected by reason. With this we should compare p. 265
D, E of the same dialogue.[2] These passages express views
of knowledge with which we would quite agree. From many
sensations we admit that we rise to a general notion, and to
divide this general notion into its subordinate genera and
species is a useful and sometimes necessary process. Had
Plato confined himself to this as a theory of knowing we
would have had no fault to find with him ; we only differ
from him when he turns the highest abstractions from modes
of knowing into modes of being. This transformation is the
essence of the Ideal theory.

VII

We may now turn to the *Symposium*, which, as I have
tried roughly to indicate, was probably written about the
same time as, though somewhat later than, the *Phaedrus*.
Its subject is the same as that of the early part of the *Phaedrus*
—love ; but of the speeches delivered on this topic only that
of Socrates [3] concerns us here. The treatment of the subject
in the *Symposium* differs from that in the *Phaedrus*, but the
two accounts may be easily reconciled. It was not Plato's
custom to exhaust a subject in one dialogue ; he loved to
present one aspect of a subject at one time, another at
another, leaving it to others to unite the two. In the speech
of Socrates, the lover, it said, should begin by loving one
beautiful form ; then seeing the similarity between all

---

[1] Given p. 249 B δεῖ γὰρ ἄνθρωπον
ξυνιέναι κατ' εἶδος λεγόμενον, ἐκ πολλῶν
ἰόντ' [ἰόντ' for ἰὸν is an almost certain
correction] αἰσθήσεων εἰς ἓν λογισμῷ

ξυναιρούμενον.

[2] εἰς μίαν τε ἰδέαν συνορῶντα ἄγειν
τὰ πολλαχῇ διεσπαρμένα κτλ.

[3] cc. 21-29, pp. 199 C-212 C.

bodily beauty, he should love all fair forms ; then he should pass upwards to beauty of the soul, he should love beautiful thoughts, laws, institutions, and so move upwards, always getting to a more and more general view of beauty, till at last he reaches Beauty itself, which is always one and the same, eternal and unchanging, completely abstract, unpolluted by such concrete rubbish [1] as flesh and colour. In the contemplation of this pure Beauty, a man should spend his life.

This account of love differs in two important particulars from that in the *Phaedrus*. First, the notion of beauty is not said to be a recollection of that Ideal beauty which we beheld in the life before birth ; the theory of ἀνάμνησις and immortality does not appear at all. In fact in speaking of men, it is said that the only immortality possible for a mortal nature is the immortality of the race, a man is immortal only by leaving descendants, who again leave descendants, and so on. (This idea is repeated by Aristotle.[2]) Secondly, whereas the lover in the *Phaedrus* adhered to one beautiful form all his life, in the *Symposium* the love of one particular person is to be only the starting-point for a generalized love of all beauty. But the two pictures may be easily united either by adding to the account in the *Symposium* the " recollection " and immortality of the *Phaedrus*, or by substituting for the particular love of the *Phaedrus* the general love of beauty of the *Symposium*.

Though the theory of ideas is not distinctly expressed in the *Symposium*, it comes out very clearly in this upward advance from particular beautiful things to the general beauty, and the terms in which the latter is described [3] leave us no room to doubt that this general beauty is the Idea of Beauty.[4] It is not corporeal,[5] it is not in any place, either in earth or heaven, and only by partaking in it do other things become beautiful.[6]

Nor is immortality of the soul denied in the *Symposium*,

---

[1] φλυαρία, p. 211 E.

[2] *De Anima* B, c. iv. p. 415 a 26-b 7.

[3] c. 39, pp. 210 E-211 E.

[4] It is αὐτὸ τὸ καλόν, p. 211 D, E (twice);

αὐτὸ τὸ θεῖον καλόν, p. 211 E ; it is ἀεὶ ὂν καὶ οὔτε γιγνόμενον οὔτε ἀπολλύμενον κτλ.

[5] P. 211 A and E.

[6] P. 211 A, B.

only immortality of bodily form. The possibility of immortality is hinted at on p. 212 A, where it is said that he who
thus spends his life in contemplating the Ideal Beauty
becomes immortal if any man does.

VIII

As I have said, the *Phaedo* probably succeeded the
Symposium. In it the Ideal theory is very fully developed
in connexion with the theory of immortality, the two being
in Plato's mind closely united. The proofs of immortality
in the *Phaedo* depend on the Ideal theory. These proofs
are divided into two great parts. In the first part (as Bonitz [1]
remarks) the Ideal theory is interwoven with and supported
by propositions drawn from the Pre-Socratic philosophy of
nature. These propositions are, first, that all growth or
change is from one opposite quality to another ; opposites
spring from and pass into their opposites. The second is,
that like is known by like ; the knowing subject must be
akin to, must resemble the object known. In the second
part of the dialogue the proof of immortality " rests exclusively on the logical consequences of the Ideal theory
itself ". [2]

In the first part the proofs given are two, and may be
summarily stated thus.

I. (*a*) It is a law of nature that all processes or changes
are transitions between contraries. Now life changes into
death ; therefore equally death must change into life : if
the former process (that from life to death) alone took
place, and the reverse (that from death to life) did not,
all things would at last be reduced to a state of death.
Therefore the soul must exist after death, since it is again
to pass into life. [3]

(*b*) Again the theory of reminiscence (which being
substantially the same as that in the *Phaedrus* and *Meno*
I need not here repeat) shows that our souls existed and
possessed intelligence before birth. [4]

---

[1] *Plat. Stud.* p. 287.
[2] Bonitz, *Pl. St.* p. 288.
[3] Pp. 70 C-72 E.
[4] Pp. 72 E-77 B.

Thus uniting (*a*) and (*b*), we find that the soul existed before birth and will exist after death, and that in that other life the soul is not only existent but intelligent.[1]

II. Only compounded things can be dissolved. The soul takes cognizance of the Ideas ; but the Ideas are simple, not compound ; and like is known by like, therefore the soul also is simple, not compound ; hence it is indissoluble and indestructible.[2]

The second part of the dialogue[3] opens with doubts raised by Simmias and Cebes as to the completeness of the proofs which have been given. Simmias' objection is that the soul may be simply the harmony of the body ; and that just as when a lute is broken, its harmony is gone, so when the body dies, the soul may perish with it. This objection is easily answered, for Simmias admits the theory of ἀνάμνησις or pre-existence ; but if the soul existed before the body, it cannot be the harmony of the body, for a harmony cannot of course exist before the thing of which it is a harmony. Moreover, we see that the soul commands the body, opposing the bodily desires ; this it could not do if it were simply the harmony of the body.

Cebes' objection is that even supposing the soul to outlast the body, it does not follow that the soul is immortal. It may outlast several bodies, passing into one after another, but it may at last be worn out itself, just as a man's body wears out a number of garments before it is itself worn out by old age or disease.[4] This objection is, after a digression in which Socrates narrates his own philosophical experience, met by an argument which also rests on the Ideal theory. The argument is in brief this. All things are what they are by participation in Ideas ; but opposite ideas cannot pass into each other, nor can a particular thing which contains one of these opposite ideas admit the contrary idea, and yet remain the thing it was. The soul has in it the Idea of life, it cannot therefore admit the Idea of death ; it is therefore immortal and indestructible.[5]

This outline of the proofs in the *Phaedo* is enough to show

[1] P. 77 B-D.
[2] Pp. 78 B-81 A.
[3] Beginning c. 35, p. 84 B.
[4] c. 37, pp. 86 E-88 B.
[5] Pp. 100 B-107 A.

that they all rest on the Ideal theory. But a more detailed examination of the dialogue is necessary.

A very remarkable feature of the dialogue [1] is the contempt expressed for the body, and the ardent wish to be rid of it. The expression of such a feeling is especially remarkable in the mouth of a Greek, seeing that no people ever had a keener sense of, and admiration for, corporeal beauty than the Greeks. But it would be a mistake to suppose that the passionate feelings here expressed are a mere transient burst of asceticism. They are based on the fundamental principles of Plato's ideal philosophy. The senses whose instruments are the bodily organs [2] do not give knowledge, they rather confuse us by the contradictions they present. For the sensible world, including the body,[3] is in constant flux, and of that which has no permanence there can be no knowledge. Knowledge is only to be attained by the pure reason apart from the body.[4] Accordingly, the soul while in the body is forced to look at reality as through prison bars.[5]

In the *Phaedo* the Ideal theory is first distinctly enounced in the second half of the first proof.[6] The proof of immortality resting on " recollection " is substantially that of the *Meno*, but the subject is discussed more fully.

Reminiscence (it is shown) [7] arises in consequence of the association of ideas, and ideas are associated on the principles either (*a*) of *resemblance* ; *e.g.* Simmias' picture suggests Simmias ; [8] or (*b*) of *contiguity* ; the lyre suggests the man in whose hands we have seen it before ; the sight of Simmias suggests the thought of Cebes, because we have seen them in contiguity ; [9] or (*c*) of *resemblance and contiguity* combined ; *e.g.* the sight of the painted lyre suggests (by resemblance) the thought of the real lyre, and that again suggests (by contiguity) the thought of the man ; Simmias' picture suggests

---

[1] Cp. especially pp. 64 A-69 E, 79 C-84 B.

[2] *Theaet.* pp. 184 B-185 E.

[3] *Sympos.* pp. 207 D, E.

[4] Cp. *Theaet.* pp. 186 B-187 A ; *Rep.* vi. p. 507 B, C to end of bk. ; *ib.* vii. c. 1, 2, 3 ; *ib.* pp. 529 B, C, D, 532 A, B, 533 A-534 E, 537 D ; x. 602 C-603 A ;

Tim. pp. 27 E-28 B, 37 A-C, 41 B-44 C, 51 B-52 C, 86 B *sqq.*

[5] *Phaedo*, p. 82 E.

[6] cc. 18-23, pp. 72 E-77 B.

[7] Pp. 73 C *sqq.*

[8] *Phaedo*, p. 73 E.

[9] P. 73 D.

(by resemblance) Simmias, and the thought of Simmias suggests (by contiguity) Cebes.[1]

In the case of mere contiguity the suggesting thought is unlike the thought suggested. Thus it appears that reminiscence is suggested by thoughts (objects) which may be either like or unlike the thought (object) suggested.[2] In all cases of reminiscence it is necessary that the idea suggested should have been in the mind before. Further, when reminiscence is suggested by resemblance, we know whether the similar (suggesting) idea or thing bears a complete or only a partial resemblance to the idea or thing which it suggests.

Now the sight of equal things (equal stones, blocks of wood, etc.) suggests the notion of equality itself. But equality itself is very different from equal things ; we see that things are never exactly equal, there is always some slight inequality between them, whereas no inequality enters into the notion of absolute equality. Now the first time we saw equal things, the sight of them suggested the notion of equality ; this notion of equality must therefore have been in our minds before we first saw equal things, since, being thus suggested by the sight of equal things, we recollected it. Whence did it come ? Not from the senses, for they only give us things which are but approximately equal. The notion of equality must therefore have been in our minds before we had our senses of sight, etc. ; but we have had our senses from the moment of birth ; we must therefore have had the notion of equality before birth ; our soul must therefore have existed before we were born into a human body. The same is true of the notions of goodness, justice, holiness, etc. ; we must have had them all before we entered on this life.[3]

This passage confirms what I maintained before, that Plato did not at first suppose Ideas of sensible substances. For in the first place, the ideas mentioned are of qualities only ; of Equality ;[4] Greater, Less, Beauty, Goodness, Justice, and Holiness in 75 C ; Beauty, Goodness καὶ πᾶσα ἡ τοιαύτη οὐσία in 76 D; Beauty and Goodness again in 77 A ; Equality and Beauty in 78 D. Again, before the theory is distinctly stated,

---

[1] P. 73 E.
[2] P. 74 A.
[3] P. 75 C, D.
[4] P. 74 A and E.

we have [1] ideas hinted at of Justice, Beauty, Goodness, Size, Health, and Strength. In c. 49, p. 100 B *sqq.*, we have Ideas of Beauty, Goodness, Greatness, Smallness, Plurality ($\pi\lambda\hat{\eta}\theta\sigma$); and in c. 52, Ideas of Heat and Cold, Odd and Even, Three, Two ; in c. 55, p. 105 D *sqq.*, there are ideas of Musicality, τὸ ἄθερμον, τὸ ἄψυκτον, Immortality (106 B), Life (106 D), and perhaps of Death (105 D). Thus in no passage in the *Phaedo* is there a hint of an Idea of a sensible substance. Again there are no Ideas laid down of Injustice, Ugliness, and (in general) of Evil. It is true that Ugliness is mentioned as the opposite of Beauty, and Injustice of Justice,[2] but when this passage is introduced, the Ideal theory has not yet been stated, and in fact in a later chapter of the dialogue [3] we are warned against supposing that the justice and injustice here spoken of are Ideas of justice and injustice. They are concrete just and unjust acts or characters, not abstract ideas of justice and injustice. Again in c. 55, p. 105 D, E we have injustice, but again it is not the Idea of injustice, but a concrete case of injustice.[4] Similarly here (105 D, E) we have not an αὐτὸ τὸ ἄδικον (Idea of Injustice), but τὸ δίκαιον μὴ δεχόμενον (a particular case of injustice), and this concrete injustice is expressed not positively as that which partakes of or admits of the Idea of Injustice, but negatively as that which does not admit the Idea of Justice. It is true that if we were to press the passage strictly it would imply an Idea of Injustice. For Plato has distinguished the Ideas from the things which admit of them, the ἰδέαι from τὰ δεχόμενα τὰς ἰδέας. Now these ἰδέαι, when (as in the case of smallness and greatness) they go in pairs of opposites, are exclusive of each other ; one of the pair of contraries cannot pass into the other, nor can the thing containing one of the contraries (*i.e.* a particular instance of the general notion) admit of the contrary idea so long as it remains what it is. Thus a particular instance of the Idea may be defined either positively from the Idea which it admits, or negatively from the Idea which it excludes. Now in the passage in which the

---

[1] P. 65 D.
[2] P. 70 E.
[3] c. 51, p. 103 A-C.
[4] Plato distinguishes them c. 50,

p. 103 B ; the Idea is αὐτὸ τὸ ἐναντίον, the concrete examples are τὰ ἔχοντα τὰ ἐναντία.

mention of injustice occurs,[1] it is Plato's object to show that the negative description Immortal (ἀθάνατον) applies to the soul. Accordingly he gives three instances of this negative denomination. These instances are: (1) that particular thing which does not admit the Idea of Even ; this thing is of course uneven (τὸ ἀνάρτιον); (2) that particular thing which does not admit the Idea of Justice ; this thing is of course unjust ; (3) τὸ ἄμουσον, ὃ ἂν μουσικὸν μὴ δέχηται (but the two former instances are sufficient for the purpose of illustration). Now, in the first of these instances, the *uneven* thing is the same as an *odd* thing ; " odd " is a positive denomination which things get [2] by admitting the Idea of Oddness. Thus we see that "uneven" here,[3] which is given as parallel to "unjust", is a mere negative name for that which has also a positive name (" odd ") by partaking in a positive Idea (Oddness). The parallel would lead us logically to infer that "unjust" is also but a negative name for that which has also a positive name by partaking in a positive Idea (the Idea of Injustice). (It is hardly necessary to point out that Injustice, like ἀδικία, is a negative name for a positive thing. Injustice is not simply the negation of Justice (for then stones and trees would strictly be unjust), but denotes the presence of certain positive evil qualities. But the fact that in Greek there is no positive name for the quality perhaps helped to make Plato overlook (as he would seem to have done) the truth that τὸ ἄδικον strictly implied a positive Idea of a certain description of evil.)

Thus I of course admit that Plato logically, even by his own words, was bound to assume ideas of injustice and of evil generally. What I hold is, not that Plato ought not logically to have assumed ideas of evil, but that as a matter of fact he did not : there is no passage in Plato where an Idea of any evil quality is indisputably laid down. The recognition that he was logically bound to assume ideas of all pairs of contrary qualities (as well when these qualities were contrasted as good and evil as when they were both in themselves indifferent) probably led Plato (as I have remarked [4])

---

[1] P. 105 D, E.
[2] As was shown, *Phaedo*, c. 52, pp. 103 E-104 B.
[3] P. 105 D.
[4] Pp. 51 *sq.*

to that abandonment, or at least great modification of, the
Ideal theory which is perceptible in his latest works.

Thus in the *Phaedo* all the Ideas without exception are
ideas of quantity or quality, not one of them is an idea of
what we call a thing or a substance. Plato expressly distinguishes the things from the qualities ; the latter *are in* the
former ; [1] the former *have* or contain the latter.[2] Thus he
distinguishes fire from the heat which it contains, snow from
the cold which it contains.[3] Again the quality in the thing
is distinct from the Idea of the quality.[4] Thus we see that
in the *Phaedo* Plato distinguishes (1) the Idea of a quality
or quantity ; (2) the quality or quantity in a particular thing ;
(3) the thing minus the quality it contains, though what that
remainder is, Plato does not here explain. Was it a collection of other qualities, shreds of other corresponding ideas ?
We must suppose that it was at least partly so. Coldness is
not the only quality of a lump of snow ; it has size, unity,
plurality (since it consists of a number of parts), it is hard
or soft, heavy or light, etc. All these qualities in the lump
of snow Plato must necessarily have explained by saying that
they were shreds of the corresponding ideas. (We know
from the *Phaedo* that he made ideas of size,[5] plurality,[6] and [7]
ideas of hardness and softness, heaviness and lightness are
hinted at.) Now did Plato suppose that the whole of each
thing was simply an aggregate of qualities derived from
ideas ? or did he believe that after deducting all the qualities
derived from ideas, there was a remainder left not to be
accounted for by the ideas ? In the earlier stage of the ideal
theory there is no trace of such a remainder, but later there
looms in the background a " vast and formless infinite ".[8]

---

1 εἶναι ἐν τῷ Σωκράτει ἀμφότερα, καὶ
μέγεθος καὶ σμικρότητα p. 102 B, τὸ ἐν
ἡμῖν μέγεθος p. 102 D, τὸ σμικρὸν τὸ ἐν
ἡμῖν E, περὶ ἐκείνων αὐτῶν ὧν ἐνόντων
ἔχει τὴν ἐπωνυμίαν τὸ ὀνομαζόμενον
p. 100 B.

2 ὃ [*scil.* μέγεθος] τυγχάνει ἔχων [ὁ
Σιμμίας] p. 102 C ; again *ib.* σμικρότητα
ἔχει ὁ Σωκράτης, again τῶν ἐχόντων τὰ
ἐναντία p. 103 B.

3 c. 52.

4 αὐτὸ τὸ μέγεθος is distinct from τὸ

ἐν ἡμῖν μέγεθος p. 102 D ; τὸ ἐν τῇ φύσει
ἐναντίον from τὸ ἐν ἡμῖν ἐναντίον 103 B.

5 cc. 49 and 50.

6 c. 49.

7 *Rep.* vii. c. 7.

8 *Timaeus*, pp. 48 E-53 C ; *Philebus*,
pp. 23 C *sqq.* It is τὸ ἄπειρον *Phil. l.c.*,
χαλεπὸν καὶ ἀμυδρὸν εἶδος *Tim.* p. 49 A,
ἀνόρατον εἶδός τε καὶ ἄμορφον *Tim.* p.
51 A, "the womb of nature", γενέσεως τιθήνην, *Tim.* p. 52 D, cp. p.
49 A, and p. 51 A τὴν τοῦ γεγονότος

This was the rough material to which the Ideas gave form, and the combination was the sensible world.[1] This shapeless matter on which the Ideas impressed form was designated in later days by Plato τὸ μέγα καὶ τὸ μικρόν.[2] But such a notion was probably not present to Plato's mind when he wrote the *Phaedo*. If questioned then, he would probably have answered that sensibles are nothing but aggregates of qualities derived from Ideas, and that Ideas are only of qualities or quantities, not of things (*i.e.* collections of qualities).

There is a remarkable passage in the *Phaedo*[3] which is of great importance for the Platonic philosophy. In it Socrates narrates his philosophical experience. A doubt might be felt whether the experience here narrated was that of the real Socrates or of Plato himself, but the fact that the development which is here described ends in the Ideal theory seems to show that the account applies to Plato. In his youth, the Platonic Socrates tells us, he had a keen desire to gain a knowledge of natural philosophy.[4] He wished to know the causes of things, why they grow and decay, and he put such questions to himself as these: Are animals generated by the union and decomposition (σηπεδόνα) of heat and cold? Is it the blood or air or fire by which we think? Or is it the brain which furnishes the senses of sight, hearing, and smell, and from the senses come memory and opinion, and from memory and opinion, when the latter has attained stability or permanence (τὸ ἠρεμεῖν), comes knowledge? He put similar questions about the destruction or decay of things, and extended his inquiries to all the phenomena of earth and heaven. But the result of these researches was so far from encouraging that it only served to show his own ignorance ; that which, before he began his investigations, he believed that he knew, he now discovered himself to be totally ignorant of. In the midst of his difficulties he heard one reading from a treatise of Anaxagoras, in which that philosopher declared that reason (νοῦς) arranges and is the cause of all

ὁρατοῦ καὶ πάντως αἰσθητοῦ μητέρα καὶ ὑποδοχήν.

[1] *Tim.* pp. 50 C-52 C.
[2] Arist. *Met.* A c. 7, 988 a 20.

[3] Pp. 96 A *sqq.*
[4] θαυμαστῶς ὡς ἐπεθύμησα ταύτης τῆς σοφίας, ἣν δὴ καλοῦσι περὶ φύσεως ἱστορίαν p. 96 A.

things.[1] This greatly pleased Socrates, who expected to find
that all things were thus arranged in the best possible way,
so that if any one wished to discover the cause of the origin,
existence, or decay of anything, he would only have to find
how it was best for the thing to arise, be, or decay. So, too,
all inquiries about human nature would be simply searches
for the highest good. He expected that Anaxagoras would
tell him, *e.g.*, whether the earth was flat or spherical, and
would then explain the cause by showing that it was better
that it should be as it is ; he hoped to learn, too, whether the
earth was in the centre of the universe or not, and if it were
in the centre that Anaxagoras would show him that it was
better that it should be so. He was prepared to put similar
questions about the sun, moon, and stars, about their relative
speeds, orbits, etc. To all these phenomena Socrates never
dreamed that Anaxagoras would think of assigning any
other cause than the fact that the existing arrangement was
the best possible.[2] He expected, moreover, to learn not only
the particular good which was the cause of each particular
thing, but the common good which was the cause of all.[3]
But when he read the book for himself his hopes were bitterly
disappointed. He found that Anaxagoras referred the order
of the world not to reason at all as a cause, but to physical
causes, air, aether, water, etc. All this, says Socrates, is
just as if a man, after saying that Socrates does everything
by virtue of his reason, were to attempt to assign the causes
of each particular act of Socrates by referring them, not to
reason, but to the physical elements of which Socrates' body
is composed. Thus, *e.g.*, he would say that the cause of
Socrates' sitting there in prison was that his body was composed of bones and sinews, that the bones are solid and fit
into each other, while the sinews can contract and relax
again ; when, then, the bones move in their sockets, the
sinews by their contraction and relaxation make the body
bend, and this (he would say) is the cause of Socrates'
sitting here. Again on the same principle, the cause of

---

[1] P. 97 B, C.

[2] οὐ γὰρ ἄν ποτε αὐτὸν ᾤμην φάσκοντά
γε ὑπὸ νοῦ αὐτὰ κεκοσμῆσθαι, ἄλλην
τινὰ αὐτοῖς αἰτίαν ἐπενεγκεῖν ἢ ὅτι

βέλτιστον αὐτὰ οὕτως ἔχειν ἐστίν, ὥσπερ
ἔχει p. 98 A.

[3] τὸ κοινὸν πᾶσιν ἐπεκδιηγήσεσθαι
ἀγαθόν.

Socrates' conversing with his friends might be said to be voice, air, sounds, etc. " The real cause " (thinks Socrates) " of my sitting and conversing here is that it seemed best to the Athenians to condemn me, and that, therefore, it seemed to me better to sit here and submit to the sentence. The physical things (bones, sinews, air, etc.) ", he continues, " are not *causes*, they are necessary conditions without which the real cause—my choice of what I deem best—could not take effect ; and it is very unphilosophical to confuse the cause with the condition." [1]   All these physical philosophers then, with their vortices, air, etc., do but grope in the dark, over-looking the true cause which binds all things together—the Good.[2]

Unable either to discover this highest cause for himself or to learn it from others, the Platonic Socrates was forced to seek for causes in the best way he could. He reflected that it was possible that he might injure himself by continually gazing (as he had been doing) on the things themselves, just as men injure their eyes by looking directly at the sun in an eclipse, instead of observing its reflection in water or some other reflecting substance. So Socrates thought that his mind might be blinded if he constantly looked at things through his eyes and other organs of sense. He accordingly resolved to study, not the things themselves, but the re-flection of them in his own mind. (He is careful, however, to point out that he believes the objects of this inward observa-tion to be quite as real as those of external observation.) The method he adopted was this. He framed an hypothesis and assumed that all that agreed with this was true, all that dis-agreed was false.[3]   But in order to the acceptance of the hypothesis, it was needful that all deductions drawn from it should be consistent.[4]   The hypothesis was to be defended, if needful, by laying down a still more general hypothesis, and that again by laying down one still more general, and so backwards, till a sufficient basis was reached.[5]   He assumed that there is an absolute Beauty, Goodness, Greatness, etc.,

[1] τὸ γὰρ μὴ διελέσθαι οἷόν τ' εἶναι ὅτι ἄλλο μέν τί ἐστι τὸ αἴτιον τῷ ὄντι, ἄλλο δ' ἐκεῖνο ἄνευ οὗ τὸ αἴτιον οὐκ ἄν ποτ' εἴη αἴτιον p. 99 B.

[2] P. 99 B, C.
[3] P. 100 A.
[4] P. 101 D.
[5] L.c.

and maintained that the cause of things being beautiful, good, great, etc., was that they partook of the absolute Beauty, etc. This, then, is the explanation of causality to which Socrates was at last driven ; of other causes he knows nothing,[1] he sticks simply to this, that the cause of a thing being beautiful is nothing but the presence of, or communion in, the absolute Beauty.[2] So with all other things ; the cause of things being great is that they partake in the absolute greatness ; of being small, that they partake in absolute smallness ; of being two that they partake in the Idea of Two.[3] In short, the Ideas are absolute existences, and all things are called what they are because they partake in these Ideas.[4]

This passage is extremely interesting and instructive as throwing light not only on Plato's philosophy, but also upon the modes of Greek thought in general, and particularly as helping to account for the acknowledged failure of the Greeks in the domain of physical science. The questions which (says Socrates) interested him in his early days referred to the causes of things, either of physical things exclusively or of physical things in relation to mind. Had Plato pursued the path by which alone he could have answered the questions which he put, he would have been a man of science instead of a philosopher, or a philosopher of nature rather than of mind. Why was he not ? At what point did he quit the path on which he had entered ? The answer is plainly given in this passage. He mistook the method and scope of physical inquiry. What a physical philosopher does is this : he puts himself in the most favourable position for watching the phenomena (this includes, of course, experiment as well as mere observation, for experiment is simply putting certain things together and then watching the phenomena which follow; the last part of an experiment is always observation); then he registers the sequence of phenomena or (to put it subjectively) of his own sensations ; then, observing that in his experience certain phenomena (sensations) have been

---

[1] οὐδὲ δύναμαι τὰς ἄλλας αἰτίας τὰς σοφὰς ταύτας γιγνώσκειν p. 100 C.

[2] ἡ ἐκείνου τοῦ καλοῦ εἴτε παρουσία εἴτε κοινωνία p. 100 D.

[3] P. 101 C.

[4] ὡμολογεῖτο εἶναί τι ἕκαστον τῶν εἰδῶν, καὶ τούτων τἆλλα μεταλαμβάνοντα αὐτῶν τούτων τὴν ἐπωνυμίαν ἴσχειν p. 102 B.

always followed by certain others, he infers that this sequence is universal, thus extending his inferences to the distant in space and time.[1] Such extended inferences are called laws of nature. They are really, however, nothing but inferences as to the sequence of our sensations ; the philosophy of nature is after all the philosophy of mind. The long and patient observation and registration of phenomena, the passive watching of sensations as they flit past, was too tedious and too unthinking a process for the fiery intellect of the Greeks ; they were too full of mental vigour to submit to being for long the passive recipients of sensations. After receiving a few sensations (observing a few phenomena) they leaped to a theory. For that long passivity which must precede the discovery of natural laws a more phlegmatic and less intellectual nature than that of the Greeks was needed, and such a nature is supplied by the northern nations. That patient observation of particulars, continued for years, nay centuries, by our men of science as a necessary preliminary to generalization, was not to be expected in a people whose blood (and therefore brain) was quickened by the more genial suns of the South. A good, we may almost say an amusing, instance of this is afforded by the present passage in Plato. He has hardly begun to watch the phenomena (if indeed he did begin at all)[2] when he rushes off to reason about them ;[3] he interrupts the chain of his sensations to raise logical questions about their data. In short, he gives up altogether the uncongenial attempt to trace the sequence of physical phenomena, and, shutting the door of his senses altogether, he locks himself up with his inner consciousness to find by lamplight the truths he had been unable to discover by the light of the sun.[4] By lamplight only ? Yes, say Locke and his school, for even as our lamps borrow their light from the sun, so is the intellect but a dimmed reflection of sense. Plato thought otherwise ; in that inner chamber,

---

[1] I am aware that this description might be pronounced inaccurate ; the sequence must be not only invariable, but (in Mill's phrase) unconditional. But this " unconditionality " is itself a result of the convergence of a number of invariable sequences ; " un-

conditionality " is but " invariability " raised to the second, third, or (according to circumstances) higher power.

[2] P. 96 A-E.

[3] Pp. 96 C *sqq.*

[4] c. 48, pp. 99 D *sqq.*

it seemed to him, there burned a light brighter than the sun, a light " that never was on sea or land ".

To decide between Plato and Locke is not for me : ἤ τοι τῆς διανοίας ὄψις ἄρχεται ὀξὺ βλέπειν, ὅταν ἡ τῶν ὀμμάτων τῆς ἀκμῆς λήγειν ἐπιχειρῇ· [ἐγώ] δὲ τούτων ἔτι πόρρω. But to return. We should notice that in the attempt to answer the questions which he had put, Plato's difficulty lay, not in selecting out of a number of antecedents those which invariably preceded, as opposed to those which did not invariably precede, the phenomena, but in applying predicates to the phenomena ; his stumbling-block was not the obscurity of the physical cause, but the logical difficulties involved in predication. For example, he wished, he says, to discover the cause of the growth of living animals, and suggests that the cause may be a sort of decomposition of heat and cold. Now instead of pursuing a course of physical observation, instead of trying to analyse an animal into its elements and these again into their elements, he observes that we call a person at first " small " and, after growth, " big " ; and so he turns aside from the observation of things to reason about the predicates we apply to them—about " smallness " and " bigness " and " unity " and " plurality ", and goodness knows what else. So his first attempt at finding the causes of things came to an untimely end ; naturally, since (like a Greek) he soon forsook physics for logic.

It did not fare much better with his second essay,[1] which was in brief an attempt to explain things by final causes. The cause why Socrates sat and talked, Plato said, was that it seemed good to him to do so ;[2] the nerves, muscles, bones, etc., which enabled him to do so were not the causes of his sitting, only the conditions,[3] that without which the act would be impossible. And if " good " is the cause of my actions, it must (Plato thought) be the cause of all things, of material things as well as of human actions. Now it is quite true that every voluntary action of every man is directed to

---

[1] cc. 46, 47, pp. 97 B-99 D.

[2] ἐμοὶ βέλτιον αὖ δέδοκται ἐνθάδε καθῆσθαι p. 98 E.

[3] ξυναίτια as opposed to αἴτια, as he afterwards distinguished physical

from final causes, *Timaeus*, p. 46 D, E, cp. *ib.* pp. 68 E-69 A χρὴ δύ' αἰτίας εἴδη διορίζεσθαι, τὸ μὲν ἀναγκαῖον, τὸ δὲ θεῖον κτλ.

some good or rather to something that seems to him good.[1] But acting thus for a good implies a mind in which there is a picture of an object to be attained. But from the fact that all our voluntary actions are prompted by this mental pre-conception of an object, were we to infer that every change in physical things is prompted by a striving after the good, we would be committing the same mistake into which savages fall when, from the analogy of their own acts, they ascribe the action of inanimate objects to a principle of life, thought, and feeling inherent in these objects. However, we cannot suppose that Plato meant to suggest anything so extravagant. He does not hint that every inanimate thing is conscious of the good to which it conduces, only that the whole system of nature is perhaps framed in such a way as ultimately to issue in the highest good. Such a theory would seem necessarily to presuppose a mind which had preconceived this supreme Good and was working it out in nature, just as men precon-ceive their particular goods and seek to attain them. The hint of the cause of all things being a final cause, that is the Good, which is here given in *Phaedo*,[2] but allowed to drop from the impossibility which Plato at the time experienced of carrying it out, is fully developed in the *Republic*. If the view be correct that there can be no Good without a mind to conceive it, this may help to throw some light on the much disputed question of the relation of God to the Ideas, and especially to the Idea of Good. Final causes can at the present stage of science be of little or no use.[3] Possibly the

[1] τοῦ γὰρ δοκοῦντος ἀγαθοῦ χάριν πάντα πράττουσι πάντες, as Aristotle says, *Pol.* i. *ad in.*, a thought borrowed, like so many of Aristotle's best thoughts, from Plato. Cp. Plato, *Rep.* p. 505 E δ [*scil.* τὸ ἀγαθὸν] διώκει μὲν ἅπασα ψυχὴ καὶ τούτου ἕνεκα πάντα πράττει; even the εἶναι δοκοῦντος of Aristotle is probably taken from Plato's *Gorgias*.

[2] Cp. p. 98 A, B ἑκάστῳ οὖν αὐτὸν ἀπο-διδόντα τὴν αἰτίαν καὶ κοινῇ πᾶσι τὸ ἑκάστῳ βέλτιστον ᾤμην καὶ τὸ κοινὸν πᾶσιν ἐπεκδιηγήσεσθαι ἀγαθόν, cp. p. 99 B-D τὴν δὲ τοῦ ὡς οἷόν τε βέλτιστα αὐτὰ τεθῆναι δύναμιν οὕτω νῦν κεῖσθαι,

ταύτην οὔτε ζητοῦσν οὔτε τινὰ οἴονται δαιμονίαν ἰσχὺν ἔχειν, ἀλλὰ ἡγοῦνται τούτου Ἄτλαντα ἄν ποτε ἰσχυρότερον καὶ ἀθανατώτερον καὶ μᾶλλον ἅπαντα ξυνέχοντα ἐξευρεῖν, καὶ ὡς ἀληθῶς τἀγαθὸν καὶ δέον ξυνδεῖν καὶ ξυνέχειν οὐδὲν οἴονται. In δέον ξυνδεῖν there is of course a conscious pun. Cp. *Cratylus*, pp. 418 E-419 B.

[3] Cp. Bacon, *Nov. Org.* i. 48 " *In-tellectus humanus—ad ulteriora ten-dens, ad proximiora recidit, videlicet ad causas finales, quae sunt plane ex natura hominis, potius quam universi: atque ex hoc fonte philosophiam miris modis corruperunt*". Cp. *ib.* p. 65, and

last discovery of science may be a final cause ; but, meanwhile, the task of the scientific discoverer is to trace the series of invariable antecedents and consequents, in other words, of physical (not final) causes and effects.

Baffled in this second attempt, Plato proceeded to make a third, which issued in the Ideal theory, this theory being thus put forward as an explanation of all physical change.[1] But how this can be represented as even an apparent answer to the questions which he had put, it is not easy to see, for while the questions referred to things (animals, the earth, sky, sun, moon, stars), in the answer only abstract qualities and quantities are explained ; while the sun, moon, and stars are left to shift for themselves. It is true that later the gate of the Ideal world was left so far ajar as to allow gross material substances such as beds and tables (or rather their disembodied spirits) to creep in, as it were, by stealth, but they were always looked at askance by their more etherial neighbours, and indeed, when some of them, such as Hair, Mud, and Dirt, presented themselves for admission, the door was shut in their face ; the line had to be drawn somewhere.[2] Thus if we asked the Socrates of the *Phaedo*, what is it that makes a thing beautiful ? he had an answer ready—the Idea of Beauty. But had we proceeded to inquire, what is it that makes a Camel ? he would not (at this stage) have been prepared to reply—the Idea of a Camel, though doubtless later the camel would have trodden the upper air like his betters, though it cost him his hump to do it. (We know [3] that there was no admission for shapes in general, much less for humps in particular.) In short, in the *Phaedo* the Ideas are made to account, not for things, but only for abstract qualities and quantities. But even in this limited region, the Ideas which

ii. 2 *causa finalis tantum abest ut prosit, ut etiam scientias corrumpat, nisi in hominis actionibus.* Cp. Descartes, *Princip. Phil.* i. 28 (under the heading, "*non causas finales rerum creatarum, sed efficientes esse examinandas*") "*Ita denique nullas unquam rationes circa res naturales, a fine, quem Deus aut natura in iis faciendis sibi proposuit, desumemus ; quia non tantum debemus nobis cor-* *rogare, ut ejus consiliorum participes nos esse putemus.*"

[1] The questions he had put were διὰ τί γίγνεται ἕκαστον καὶ διὰ τί ἀπόλλυται καὶ διὰ τί ἔστι ; and the final answer to these questions was the Ideal theory, pp. 100 A *sqq.*

[2] *Parmen.* p. 131 B.

[3] From *Crat.* p. 424 and *Phaedr.* p. 247 C.

Plato called causes we would rather call effects, for we are accustomed to regard abstractions (as the name indicates) as derived from things, not (as Plato did) to regard things as derived from abstractions. Thus it is impossible for us to accept the Platonic theory of causation, because it depends on Plato's fundamental error, the bestowal of objective existence on subjective abstractions.

Since the days when mediaeval Realism finally disappeared, the question with regard to general notions which has occupied philosophers has been, not their objective existence, but the form which they assume in our minds. Can we picture to our imagination the general notion of a man or of a triangle ? Locke thought we could, though with some difficulty.[1] This, the conceptualist view, was rejected by Locke's followers, Berkeley and Hume, who hold that a general notion is simply the notion of a particular case regarded as standing for or representing all similar cases, that (in the words of Berkeley) [2] " an Idea which, considered in itself, is particular, becomes general by being made to represent or stand for all other particular ideas of the same sort ". This conclusion Hume [3] supports by various arguments. This view, in fact, denies that there are any general notions conceived by the mind at all. This is of course the Nominalist view. It is adopted by Mill. " General concepts, therefore," he says,[4] " we have, properly speaking, none ; we have only complex ideas of objects in the concrete : but we are able to attend exclusively to certain parts of the concrete idea : and by that exclusive attention we enable those parts to determine exclusively the course of our thoughts as subsequently called up by association ; and we are in a condition to carry on a train of meditation or reasoning relating to those parts only, exactly as if we were able to conceive them separately from the rest." On the other hand, it might perhaps be maintained that we have general notions though we cannot depict them to the imagination. This distinction between thought which is and thought which is not, capable of being depicted by the imagination,

---

[1] *Essay on Hum. Underst.* bk. iv. c. 7, § 9.
[2] Introd. to *Princip. of Human Knowledge*, § 12.
[3] *Treatise of Human Nature*, bk. i. pt. i. sect. vii.
[4] *Exam. of Hamilton*, p. 321.

was made by Descartes (I forget where the passage occurs, and it is hardly worth the trouble of ransacking him to discover); as an example of the latter kind of thought he gives the notion of a figure of 1000 sides. No one can picture such a figure to his imagination, but every civilized man has a notion of what it is. (I say civilized man, for savages are, it is well known, often deficient in their notions of number, not altogether, but in degrees varying according to their intelligence and progress.) Now it might possibly be maintained of general notions in a similar way, that though we cannot picture them to the imagination, yet they really exist as notions of the understanding.

It is almost idle to ask which, if any, of these views Plato adopted, for he was so thorough a Realist that the objective form and reality of the ideas occupied his attention almost exclusively, while he hardly looked at the subjective side so far as to ask what form the conceptions of these objective ideas take in our minds. Indeed he can hardly be said to have distinguished the objective idea from our subjective conception of it; the latter disappeared in the former, or rather the former was merely the latter viewed as outside the mind. However, there is one point we can be quite certain of; he did not, like the Nominalists, regard the Idea as a particular which represents all other similar particulars. This is proved, e.g., by the passages in the present dialogue in which he repeatedly and emphatically insists that Equality in general (αὐτὸ τὸ ἴσον) is different from all particular equal things.[1] From this it follows that in Plato's view the conception of equality is different from the conception of any particular equal thing. This view is supported by *Cratylus*, c. 34, from which we learn that the εἶδος of a thing was distinct from its shape, colour, and sound, i.e. from its sensible qualities generally. Compare too *Phaedrus*, p. 247 C, which agrees with the passage just cited from the *Cratylus* in describing the essence of things (i.e. the Ideas) as colourless, formless, and intangible. Thus if the Platonic Ideas are merely general notions made objective, at least it is not the conceptions of particulars regarded as representative which are thus made objective. Indeed, had

[1] Pp. 74 B, C, D, E, 75 A, B.

he held the Nominalist view, his Ideal theory would have had no standing ground ; what we call general notions would then have been for him nothing but repetitions of sensible particulars, representations of the presentations of sense ; all our knowledge would then have come from sense. There would have been no ideas derived from above, independent of sense ; all would have come from below.

Aristotle did put to himself the question which Plato had failed to ask, how we conceive general notions, and he characteristically answered it distinctly in the same way as Berkeley and Mill do.[1]

I had intended to examine in equal detail the later dialogues in which Plato expands and modifies his theory of Ideas, but the results reached by the preceding investigations are not sufficiently encouraging to induce me to carry out the plan. Moreover, " *Sol me ille admonuit ut brevior essem* ", for he is already far on his way to the South. I shall therefore content myself with a much more summary review of the later dialogues. And first of the *Republic*.

IX

In the *Republic* the theory is made much more definite and complete both on the objective and subjective sides. The objective world is divided into three regions, (1) the Existent (ὄν) ; (2) the Non-Existent (μὴ ὄν) ; (3) that which is at the same time both Existent and Non-Existent, and hence holds a position intermediate between the two former regions.[2] Corresponding to these three objective regions, there are three subjective states or faculties : (1) corresponding to Existence is Knowledge ;[3] (2) corresponding to Non-Existence is Ignorance ;[4] (3) corresponding to the intermediate region is Opinion.[5] The intermediate

---

[1] *De Mem.* 449 b 30 *ap.* Trendelenberg on Arist. *de An.* pp. 143-144, 2nd ed. Grote, *Aristotle*, v. ii. p. 226 note, notices the exact coincidence of Aristotle and Berkeley, and quotes a parallel passage from the latter.

[2] ἅμα ὄν τε καὶ μὴ ὄν,—τὸ ἀμφο-τέρων μετέχον, τοῦ εἶναί τε καὶ μὴ εἶναι. *Rep.* v. pp. 476 E-477 A, 478 D, E.

[3] γνῶσις pp. 477 A, 478 C or ἐπιστήμη p. 478 A and D.

[4] ἀγνωσία p. 477 A, ἄγνοια p. 478 C and D.

[5] δόξα, p. 478 D.

region consists of the sensible world, with its multitude of beautiful things, large things, heavy things, etc. These things are, when viewed in one light, beautiful, large, heavy, etc. ; when viewed in another they are ugly, small, light, etc. ; thus they both are and are not beautiful, large, heavy, etc. ; hence (Plato inferred, though wrongly) they both are and are not : therefore they are intermediate between Existence and Non-Existence, and are apprehended by Opinion, which is a faculty inferior to Knowledge (which deals with Existence) but superior to Ignorance.[1] Existence is γνωστόν (p. 477 A), Non-Existence is ἄγνωστον (ib.), the Intermediate is δοξαστόν (p. 479 D).

In the sixth book this division of the objective world into distinct regions and of the knowing subject into corresponding faculties is carried out with still greater fullness. The whole objective universe is divided into two great regions (identical with the first and third of the above regions ; in the sixth book the purely Non-Existent is left out of account).

I. The ὁρατόν, ὁρώμενον or sensible region.

II. The νοητόν, νοούμενον, or intelligible region.[2] Each of these is subdivided into two regions ; the sensible into (a) Images, εἰκόνες (reflections, shadows, etc.),[3] and (b) animals, and all inanimate objects whether natural or artificial.[4] The Intelligible region is subdivided into (a) pure mathematics and (b) Ideas. These four classes of objects are apprehended by four mental faculties : Ideas by ἐπιστήμη, Mathematics by διάνοια, Sensible things by πίστις, Images by εἰκασία. The two first faculties together constitute νόησις, the two latter δόξα : the objects of the two former faculties taken together constitute οὐσία ; those of the two latter γένεσις. The former objects, in relation to the faculty which apprehends them, are νοητόν ; the latter objects, in relation to the faculty which apprehends them, are δοξαστόν.[5]

---

[1] P. 478 C, D.

[2] P. 509 D.

[3] Pp. 509 E-510 A,

[4] τά τε περὶ ἡμᾶς ζῶα καὶ πᾶν τὸ φυτευτὸν καὶ τὸ σκευαστὸν ὅλον γένος p. 510 A.

[5] I have here followed the nomen-clature of Rep. vii. pp. 533 C-534 A, which is fuller and more precise than that given at the close of Rep. vi. In the latter book, p. 511 D, what I (following Rep. vii.) have called ἐπιστήμη is designated νοῦς and νόησις. Also ἡ τοῦ διαλέγεσθαι δύναμις p. 511 B

The distinction between the two higher faculties (νοῦς or ἐπιστήμη and διάνοια) is that the latter sets out from hypotheses and works from them downwards deductively to the conclusions ; the other, νοῦς, starts also from hypotheses, but instead of assuming the truth of these hypotheses throughout and deducing conclusions from them without examining these its premises, it works backwards from these hypotheses to a first principle (ἀρχή) or rather to the first principle of all things (τὴν τοῦ παντὸς ἀρχήν),[1] and then from this first principle it works downwards to its conclusions. Again διάνοια uses as its instruments sensible things,[2] though its reasonings apply not to the visible diagrams but to the purely intelligible squares, etc. ; [3] whereas νοῦς employs only Ideas throughout, without using sensible things at all.[4]

The precision thus given to the theory both on its objective and subjective sides is perhaps the chief advance made in the *Republic*. There are, besides, two other notable features in the doctrine as it is represented in the *Republic*, which cannot, even in a summary review, be omitted. These are, first, the supremacy assigned in the world of Ideas to the Idea of the Good in Books VI. and VII., and, secondly, the creation of the Ideas by God in Book X. But before adverting to these two points, it may be more convenient to inquire whether in the *Republic* Plato makes Ideas of all things which are united by a common name, especially whether he assumes Ideas (*a*) of material substances, such as horse, house ; and (*b*) of Injustice, and generally of Evil.

In order to answer this question, I shall collect those Ideas which Plato either distinctly assumes or at least implies.

In *Republic* v. pp. 475 E-476 A we have καλόν and αἰσχρόν, δίκαιον and ἄδικον, ἀγαθόν and κακόν spoken of as opposites and as εἴδη, each one in itself though each appears to be

and ἡ τοῦ διαλέγεσθαι ἐπιστήμη p. 511 C. But it is more symmetrical to retain νόησις to include both ἐπιστήμη (or νοῦς) and διανοία, just as δόξα includes both πίστις and εἰκασία.

[1] Which first principle is not hypothetical, pp. 510 B, 511 B.

[2] τοῖς τότε τμηθεῖσιν ὡς εἰκόσι χρωμένη

p. 510 B.

[3] τοῦ τετραγώνου αὐτοῦ ἕνεκα τοὺς λόγους ποιούμενοι καὶ διαμέτρου αὐτῆς, ἀλλ' οὐ ταύτης ἣν γράφουσι κτλ. p. 510 D.

[4] ἐπὶ τελευτὴν καταβαίνῃ αἰσθητῷ παντάπασιν οὐδενὶ προσχρώμενος, ἀλλ' εἴδεσιν αὐτοῖς δὲ αὐτῶν εἰς αὐτά, καὶ τελευτᾷ εἰς εἴδη p. 511 B, C.

many in the world of sense.¹ This is the strongest evidence
that can be adduced in support of the view that Plato assumed
Ideas of Vice. I have already, however, tried to show ² that
the passage is not so decisive as it at first sight appears to be.
The use of the term εἶδος is not of course conclusive, since
Plato uses it in so many various senses. Just a little below ³
τὸ εἶδος denotes a class, without any of its technical sense.⁴
On the same page, immediately after the passage quoted
above, the Idea of Beauty is mentioned four times,⁵ as opposed
to beautiful things.⁶ But here, as elsewhere, there is no
mention of the opposite αὐτὸ τὸ αἰσχρόν or αὐτὴ αἰσχρότης
by participation in which ugly things are ugly.

Further down ⁷ we have Ideas of Beauty and Justice,
αὐτὸ καλόν, ἰδέα αὐτοῦ κάλλους (opposed to τὰ πολλὰ καλά);
ἐν τὸ καλὸν καὶ δίκαιον καὶ τἆλλα οὕτω. Then he proceeds
to oppose to these Ideas the particulars of sense. The πολλὰ
καλά are also αἰσχρά, the δίκαια are also ἄδικα, the ὅσια ἀνόσια,
the διπλάσια ἡμίσεα, the μεγάλα σμικρά, the κοῦφα βαρέα.
But here again he does not speak of Ideas of ugliness or
injustice (only of particular ugly and unjust things), though
he had just spoken of Ideas of Justice and Goodness.

P. 479 D, E, we have Ideas of Beauty and Justice (αὐτὸ τὸ
καλόν, αὐτὸ τὸ δίκαιον) as opposed to the particulars (πολλὰ
καλά, πολλὰ δίκαια).

In *Republic* vi. 481 D we have ἡ τοῦ ὄντος ἰδέα, which
is a general description of all the Ideas.

On p. 493 E, Idea of Beauty αὐτὸ καλόν opposed to the
particulars τὰ πολλὰ καλά.

P. 500 B, Ideas of Justice, Beauty, Temperance, and " all
such things", τὸ φύσει δίκαιον καὶ καλὸν καὶ σῶφρον καὶ πάντα
τὰ τοιαῦτα. (This whole passage, c. xiii. pp. 500 B-501 C, is
utterly inconsistent with the notion that there were Ideas of
evil. The philosopher is here said to stand apart from the
contests of men, to be free from their jealousies and enmities ;

---

¹ πάντων τῶν εἰδῶν πέρι ὁ αὐτὸς
λόγος, αὐτὸ μὲν ἐν ἕκαστον εἶναι, τῇ δὲ
τῶν πράξεων καὶ σωμάτων καὶ ἀλλήλων
κοινωνίᾳ πανταχοῦ φανταζόμενα πολλὰ
φαίνεσθαι ἕκαστον p. 476 A.
² P. 50.
³ P. 477 E.

⁴ Cp. Campbell, Appendix C, to
his edit. of the *Theaetetus*.
⁵ αὐτοῦ τοῦ καλοῦ—αὐτὸ τὸ καλόν—
αὐτὸ κάλλος—αὐτὸ καλόν.
⁶ καλὰ πράγματα, τὰ ἐκείνου [*scil.*
αὐτοῦ τοῦ καλοῦ] μετέχοντα.
⁷ P. 479 A.

he gazes εἰς τεταγμένα ἄττα καὶ κατὰ ταῦτα ἀεὶ ἔχοντα—οὔτ'
ἀδικοῦντα οὔτ' ἀδικούμενα ὑπ' ἀλλήλων κόσμῳ δὲ πάντα καὶ
κατὰ λόγον ἔχοντα, and imitates the Ideas and makes himself
like to them (ἀφομοιοῦσθαι) as far as possible. A pretty
character would result from imitating Ideas of Injustice,
Cowardice, Intemperance, etc. On the contrary, the philosopher (Plato continues) by associating with the divine and
orderly becomes himself orderly and divine as far as man can.
Further, he tries to introduce amongst mankind what he sees
in the Ideal world (ἃ ἐκεῖ ὁρᾷ), and to make men conform to
the Ideas, and in so doing, ἆρα κακὸν δημιουργὸν αὐτὸν οἴει
γενήσεσθαι σωφροσύνης τε καὶ δικαιοσύνης καὶ ξυμπάσης τῆς
δημοτικῆς ἀρετῆς; to which the answer is ἥκιστά γε. All
this, and more of the same sort, seems to make the notion of
Ideas of evil untenable.)

P. 505 A, we have the Idea of the Good, ἡ τοῦ ἀγαθοῦ ἰδέα.

P. 507 B, Ideas of Beauty and Goodness (αὐτὸ καλόν and
αὐτὸ ἀγαθόν) as opposed to πολλὰ καλά and πολλὰ ἀγαθά.

P. 510 E, Ideas of a Square and a Diagonal (τοῦ τετραγώνου
αὐτοῦ—διαμέτρου αὐτῆς) as opposed to those of sense (τοῖς
ὁρωμένοις εἴδεσι—ταῦτα ἃ πλάττουσί τε καὶ γράφουσι).

In Book VII. p. 517 B, Idea of the Good (ἡ τοῦ ἀγαθοῦ
ἰδέα), ib. of Justice (αὐτὴ δικαιοσύνη). Again (to omit one
or two mentions of the Good), p. 520 C, Ideas of Beauty,
Justice, and Goodness are hinted at in contrast to their
phantoms (εἴδωλα, i.e. counterparts in the sensible world).

Pp. 523 E-524 C, Ideas are hinted at of Small and Great,
Thick and Thin, Soft and Hard, Light and Heavy.

Pp. 524 E and 525 E, Idea of One (αὐτὸ τὸ ἕν), and of
Numbers generally (αὐτῶν τῶν ἀριθμῶν) in p. 525 D.

P. 526 E, Idea of Good (τὴν τοῦ ἀγαθοῦ ἰδέαν).

P. 529, Ideas of Speed and Slowness, Numbers and Form
(τὸ ὂν τάχος καὶ ἡ οὖσα βραδυτὴς ἐν τῷ ἀληθινῷ ἀριθμῷ καὶ
πᾶσι τοῖς ἀληθέσι σχήμασι).

P. 531 C, Ideas of Beauty and Goodness (hinted at).[1]

---

[1] *N.B.*—The αὐτὰ τὰ ζῶα and αὐτὰ
ἄστρα and αὐτὸν τὸν ἥλιον of p.
532 A are not, as they might at first
appear to be, Ideas of animals, stars,
and sun; they are sensible, substantial animals, as opposed to the
shadows which the prisoners saw in
the cave. The whole passage. p.
532 A-D, puts this beyond a doubt.
Plato is describing dialectic and
illustrating it by the allegory of the
cave. Compare especially p. 532 C

Idea of Good, p. 532 A (αὐτὸ ὃ ἔστιν ἀγαθόν).
Idea of Good, p. 534 B, C (τὴν τοῦ ἀγαθοῦ ἰδέαν—αὐτὸ τὸ ἀγαθόν).
Ideas of Beauty, Justice, and Goodness (hinted at), p. 538 D, E.
Idea of the Good, p. 540 A (τὸ ἀγαθὸν αὐτό).

Such are the Ideas either expressly mentioned or at least hinted at in the *Republic* (to omit for the present Book X., to which I shall refer presently). The enumeration of these passages supports my conclusions (1) that there were no Ideas of Evil, and (2) that for a long time Plato did not assume ideas of material substances. For in the long list given above, there is certainly no Idea of a sensible substance, and (with one doubtful exception) no idea of any vice. It might be said that the allegory of the cave, with its mention of articles of all kinds and figures of men and of other animals,[1] implies Ideas of all sensible things, or at least of all classes of sensible things. But this by no means follows ; the whole passage is a mere illustration ; Plato does not hint that he makes the Ideal world a mere double of this lower, as the poet Fracastorius [2] seems to have supposed that he did.

An nescis, quaecunque heic sunt, quae hac nocte teguntur
Omnia res prorsus veras non esse, sed umbras,
Aut specula, unde ad nos aliena elucet imago ?
Terra quidem, et maria alta, atque his circumfluus aer,
Et quae consistunt ex his, haec omnia tenueis
Sunt umbrae, humanos quae tanquam somnia quaedam
Pertingunt animos, fallaci et imagine ludunt,
Nunquam eadem, fluxu semper variata perenni.
Sol autem, Lunaeque globus, fulgentiaque astra
Caetera, sint quamvis meliori praedita vita,
Et donata aevo immortali, haec ipsa tamen sunt
Aeterni specula, in quae animus, qui est inde profectus,
Inspiciens, patriae quodam quasi tactus amore,
Ardescit. Sed enim, quoniam heic non perstat, et ultra

πᾶσα αὕτη ἡ πραγματεία τῶν τεχνῶν ἃς διήλθομεν, ταύτην ἔχει τὴν δύναμιν καὶ ἐπαναγωγὴν τοῦ βελτίστου ἐν ψυχῇ πρὸς τὴν τοῦ ἀρίστου ἐν τοῖς οὖσι θέαν, ὥσπερ τότε τοῦ σαφεστάτου **ἐν σώματι** πρὸς τὴν τοῦ φανοτάτου **ἐν τῷ σωματο-ειδεῖ τε καὶ ὁρατῷ τόπῳ**, where the τοῦ σαφεστάτου ἐν σώματι is ἡ τῆς

ὄψεως δύναμις (p. 352 A, cp. *Phaedo*, p. 65 B, *Phaedr.* p. 250 D), and the τοῦ φανοτάτου ἐν τῷ σωματοειδεῖ τε καὶ ὁρατῷ τόπῳ is the αὐτὸν τὸν ἥλιον referred to above, p. 532 A.

[1] Pp. 514 E-515 A.
[2] Quoted by Hamilton, *Lectures on Metaphysics*. ii. pp. 33, 34.

Nescio quid sequitur secum, tacitusque requirit,
Nosse licet circum haec ipsum consistere verum
Non finem : verum esse aliud quid, cuius imago
Splendet in iis, quod per se ipsum est, et principium esse
Omnibus aeternum, ante omnem numerumque diemque ;
In quo alium Solem atque aliam splendescere Lunam
Adspicias, aliosque orbes, alia astra manere,
Terramque, fluviosque alios, atque aera, et ignem,
Et nemora, atque aliis errare animalia silvis.

Indeed, not only is this theory of the Ideal being but a glorified double of the sensible world, not a necessary deduction from the illustration, but it is not even reconcilable with the application Plato himself makes of the allegory. For on this hypothesis the sun of the Ideal world must have been an Idea of Sun, whereas it was really the Idea of Good.[1] So that if we follow out the line which Plato has himself indicated, we must suppose that the Ideas were Ideas, not of concrete things (sun, moon, stars, table, house, etc.), but of abstractions (goodness, beauty, etc.).

Now for the tenth book. Here we have it most unquestionably laid down that there are ideas of all classes of things which have common names,[2] and ideas are mentioned of those very substantial things, beds and tables. Here, then, at last, Plato has given in to logical requirements. He has assumed in general an idea corresponding to every class name, and has carried this principle into practice so far as to assume ideas of concrete things (a length to which he had not gone before), but he does not carry his logical consistency so far as to assume ideas of vice and of evil generally.

Thus in the exposition of the Ideal theory in Books V., VI., and VII., not only is there no mention made of Ideas of concrete things, but the supposition of such ideas is, strictly, inconsistent with Plato's own illustration of the cave. Accordingly the fact that such ideas are distinctly assumed in the tenth book gives some support to the view of Hermann, that the tenth book was written later than the rest of the *Republic*, for it certainly was not till his later days that Plato made ideas of material substances.

---

[1] *Rep.* vii. pp. 517 B, C, 518 C, D,   τίθεσθαι περὶ ἕκαστα τὰ πολλά, οἷς
cp. vi. pp. 506 D-509 D.   ταὐτὸν ὄνομα ἐπιφέρομεν p. 596 A.

[2] εἶδος γάρ ποι' τι ἐν ἕκαστον εἰώθαμεν

The list of Ideas given above may help to confirm my conjecture, that Plato started the Ideal theory primarily to explain, not our general notions as a whole, but only those which have not a sensible counterpart, but above all to explain those moral notions on which Socrates had dwelt with so much emphasis. Hence the constant repetition of the Ideas of Beauty (which included moral notions for the Greeks), Goodness, and Justice.

The supremacy assigned to the Idea of Good is the second great feature which distinguishes the representation of the Ideal theory given in the *Republic* from those of previous (and, indeed, of subsequent) dialogues. In previous dialogues the Idea of Good was simply one of the world of Ideas, to which it is not represented as superior.[1] The analogy by which in the *Republic*[2] Plato seeks to explain the superiority of the Good to everything else is this. The Sun is, he says, the offspring of the Good, and its representative in the visible world. In the visible world we have (1) the sun ; (2) objects of sight ; (3) the eye ; (4) light, which coming from the sun imparts (*a*) to the eye the power of seeing ; (*b*) to the objects of sight the power of being seen, and not only the power of being seen, but (*c*) birth, growth, and nourishment. So in the intelligible world we have (1) the Idea of Good ; (2) the objects of Reason, or Ideas ; (3) Reason ; (4) (*a*) Knowledge, which is imparted by the Idea of Good to Reason, as the power of seeing is imparted by the light of the sun to the eye ; (*b*) Truth, which is imparted by the Idea of Good to the objects of Reason or Ideas, as the power of being seen is imparted by the light of the sun to the objects of sight ; and (*c*) Being, which is imparted by the Idea of Good to Ideas, as birth, growth, and nourishment are imparted by the light of the sun to the objects of sight.

Thus the Idea of Good is the source of all Knowledge, Truth, and Being ; it itself is none of these, but superior to them all. It is the source of all existence whatever, not only in the Ideal, but also in the sensible world, for it created the sun,[3] and the sun is the nourisher of all the rest of the sensible world.[4]

---

[1] Cp., *e.g. Phaedo*, pp. 75 C, 100 B ;
Crat. pp. 439 C, 440 C.
    Pp. 507 *sqq.*

[3] P. 508 B.
[4] P. 509 B.

I have already[1] offered a suggestion as to the train of
thought by which Plato was led to this position, and need
not here repeat it.

The last great feature of the theory in the *Republic*
appears in Book X. (The reasons which shorten this essay
induce or compel me to pass over the account in Book VII.
of the studies which lead up to dialectic. They are all
mathematical—for even astronomy and music are to be
studied as based on pure mathematics—and are thus intended
to develop the διάνοια in order to prepare for the full exercise
of the νοῦς in dialectic, or the contemplation of pure Ideas.)
In *Republic* x. p. 597 God is represented as the maker of
the Idea of Bed, and as Plato had said just before (p. 596 A),
that there were Ideas of all classes of things bearing a common
name, it must of course be intended that God was the Creator
of all the Ideas.

The disputed question of the relation of God to the
Ideas, either as the Creator of them all, or as identical with
the Idea of Good, or as containing them all in His own
mind, etc., I have neither the inclination nor the ability to
discuss. It is enough to state the fact that when Plato
wrote the tenth book of the *Republic* he believed that the
Ideas were the creation of God. It is worth while noticing
that in the earlier books, though Plato does not speak of
God as Creator of the Ideas, yet he twice makes use of
expressions which point to a belief in a personal creator.[2]
The same word δημιουργός is used in the *Timaeus* to denote
the Creator of the world who is there certainly spoken of,
not as the Idea of Good, but as God. We should notice, too,
the passage[3] where God is described as the cause, not of
all things, but only of the good. On the whole, we may say
that the question as to the relation in Plato's mind between
God and the Ideas, especially the Idea of Good, cannot
be answered, because the Platonic writings do not supply

[1] P. 51.
[2] These expressions are *Rep.* vi.
p. 507 C ἆρ᾽ οὖν, ἦν δ᾽ ἐγώ, ἐννενόηκας
τὸν τῶν αἰσθήσεων δημιουργὸν ὅσῳ
πολυτελεστάτην τὴν τοῦ ὁρᾶν τε καὶ
ὁρᾶσθαι δύναμιν ἐδημιούργησεν; and
vii. p. 530 A τῷ ὄντι δὴ ἀστρονομικόν,

ἦν δ᾽ ἐγώ, ὄντα οὐκ οἴει ταὐτὸν πεί-
σεσθαι εἰς τὰς τῶν ἄστρων φορὰς ἀπο-
βλέποντα; νομιεῖν μὲν ὡς οἷόν τε
κάλλιστα τὰ τοιαῦτα ἔργα συστήσασθαι
οὕτω ξυνεστάναι τῷ τοῦ οὐρανοῦ δημι-
ουργῷ αὐτόν τε καὶ τὰ ἐν αὐτῷ.
[3] In *Rep.* ii. p. 379.

materials for judging. The view of Schwegler is perhaps most consistent with the facts as we find them. " The probability is, then, that he never definitely put to himself the entire question of the personality of God ; that he allowed himself to entertain the religious idea of God as his own natural conviction ; that, in an ethical interest, he even vindicated it as against the anthropomorphism of the mythological poets (*Republic, Laws*) ; that he attempted to establish it from the facts of design in nature and of a universally diffused belief in God (*Laws*) ; but that philosophically he made no use of it." [1]

The fact that in the tenth book God is spoken of as the Creator of the Ideas, whereas in the earlier books He is not mentioned at all in connexion with them, seems (taken along with the mention of Ideas of concrete things in Book X.) to favour Hermann's view that the tenth book was composed after the others. For both these points are characteristic of the later phase of the Ideal theory. The reference to God is especially to be compared with the δημιουργός of the *Timaeus* and the νοῦς which is the αἰτία of the *Philebus*.

X

The subject of the *Timaeus* is described in the words of Critias, p. 27 A λέγειν ἀρχομένον ἀπὸ τῆς τοῦ κόσμου γενέσεως, τελευτᾶν δὲ εἰς ἀνθρώπων φύσιν. Timaeus, on whom this task devolves, begins by distinguishing that which always is from that which is always becoming ; the former is apprehended by reason and is ever the same, the latter is the object of opinion, and is ever coming into being and perishing.[2] Further the latter, the Becoming or Generated, must have had a cause, it must have been generated by something. Now this universe or world [3] belongs to the class of the Becoming or Generated, since it is corporeal, visible, and tangible. It must therefore have had (like all

---

[1] Schwegler, p. 81, Eng. tr.

[2] πρῶτον διαιρετέον τάδε· τί τὸ ὂν ἀεί, γένεσιν δὲ οὐκ ἔχον, καὶ τί τὸ γιγνόμενον μὲν ἀεί, ὂν δὲ οὐδέποτε; τὸ μὲν δὴ νοήσει μετὰ λόγου περιληπτὸν ἀεὶ κατὰ ταὐτὰ ὄν, τὸ δ' αὖ δόξῃ μετ' αἰσθήσεως ἀλόγου δοξαστόν, γιγνόμενον καὶ ἀπολλύμενον, ὄντως δὲ οὐδέποτε ὄν pp. 27 D-28 A.

[3] ὁ δὴ πᾶς οὐρανὸς ἢ κόσμος ἢ καὶ ἄλλο ὅ τι ποτε ὀνομαζόμενος μάλιστ' ἂν δέχοιτο, τοῦθ' ἡμῖν ὠνομάσθω p. 28 B.

generated things) a cause. Without trying to discover and
explain what this cause is (which he says it would be hard
to do),¹ Timaeus immediately proceeds to speak of the cause
in the masculine gender as if it were a person, ὁ τεκταινόμενος,
and afterwards as ὁ δημιουργός (p. 29 A), as ὁ ξυνιστὰς τοδὲ
τὸ πᾶν (p. 29 D), and similarly throughout the dialogue.
Now this personal cause Plato describes constantly as God.²
Thus there is no doubt that in the *Timaeus* the Creator or
producer of the sensible universe is represented (at least
popularly) as God.

Timaeus proceeds to inquire on what model the Creator ³
fashioned the universe : did the Model belong to the first
or second class, to the eternally Existent and Unchangeable
(τὸ κατὰ ταὐτὰ καὶ ὡσαύτως ἔχον), or to the Becoming or
Generated (τὸ γεγονός)? Timaeus decides that the Creator
used the Eternal model (τὸ ἀΐδιον, p. 29 A). The Model is
παράδειγμα, the universe is its image εἰκών (p. 29 B). Now
it can be shown that this Model was an Idea. It has the
attributes which Plato is in the habit of ascribing to Ideas.
It belongs to the former of the two classes, the τὸ—νοήσει μετὰ
λόγου περιληπτὸν ἀεὶ κατὰ ταὐτὰ ὄν p. 28 A, cp. p. 29 A τὸ
ἀΐδιον, τὸ λόγῳ καὶ φρονήσει περιληπτὸν καὶ κατὰ ταὐτὰ ἔχον.
This Idea is the Ideal animal. For God, knowing that the
rational is better than the irrational and that reason can
only exist where there is life, made the universe a living
animal. The Model was not any particular animal, but
that animal of which all other animals, both as individuals
and as classes, are but parts, that animal, namely, which
comprehends the notions of all animals in itself.⁴ This
all-comprehending animal is undoubtedly the Ideal Animal.
This is confirmed by what immediately follows, p. 29 A, B.

---

¹ τὸν μὲν οὖν ποιητὴν καὶ πατέρα
τοῦδε τοῦ παντὸς εὑρεῖν τε ἔργον καὶ
εὑρόντα εἰς πάντας ἀδύνατον λέγειν p.
28 C.

² See pp. 30 A, B, E, 31 B, 32 B, 34
A, C, 38 C (twice), 39 B, 46 C, E, 47 B, 53
B, 55 C, 69 B, 71 A, 73 B, 90 A, 92 A.

³ The word creator is rather in-
exact. The word, with us, conveys
the sense of producing something
out of nothing. The δημιουργός of

the *Timaeus* is only represented as
reducing chaos to order.

⁴ λεκτέον τινὶ τῶν ζώων αὐτὸν εἰς
ὁμοιότητα ὁ ξυνιστὰς ξυνέστησε. τῶν
μὲν οὖν ἐν μέρους εἶδει πεφυκότων
μηδενὶ καταξιώσωμεν· ἀτελεῖ γὰρ ἐοικὸς
οὐδέν ποτ' ἂν γένοιτο καλόν· οὗ δ' ἔστι
τἆλλα ζῷα καθ' ἓν καὶ κατὰ γένη μόρια,
τούτῳ πάντων ὁμοιότατον αὐτὸν εἶναι
τιθῶμεν. τὰ γὰρ δὴ νοητὰ ζῷα πάντα
ἐκεῖνο ἐν ἑαυτῷ περιλαβὸν ἔχει.

It is there said that there is but one sensible universe, since
the Model which comprehends all intelligible animals is also
single. Now we know from *Republic* x. p. 597 C that there
was only one Idea of each kind (*e.g.* one Idea of Bed), and
the reasons assigned in the *Republic* and *Timaeus* for the
singleness of the Ideas are identical, constituting in fact an
attempt to obviate the τρίτος ἄνθρωπος argument.

If any doubt remained as to whether the Model on which
God fashioned the world was or was not an Idea, it would
be removed by the passage [1] in which the whole subject of
the relation of the Ideas to the sensible universe is discussed.
This passage is very important for the subject in hand, as in
it a very great step is made in the development of the Ideal
theory, and one of which we have had as yet no hint in
Plato. I refer to the announcement of the τρίτον γένος,
the so-called Platonic matter. Previously, says Timaeus
(p. 48 E), we distinguished only two classes, one the eternally
existent and unchangeable, the Model ; the other, the Imitation of the Model, generated and visible.[2] We must, however (he proceeds), add a third class, dim and difficult to
describe (χαλεπὸν καὶ ἀμυδρὸν εἶδος). This is in brief a
substrate (ὑποκείμενον in its Aristotelian metaphysical, not
of course, logical sense)[3] which, in itself, formless, admits
of all forms. These forms come from without and are impressed on this substrate as on a plastic substance. (This
comparison occurs, p. 50 E, and other illustrations are used
to explain the notion.) A great variety of phrases are em-
ployed to describe this substrate.[4] It is not earth, air, fire,
or water (p. 51 A), it is without form (ἄμορφον pp. 50 D, 51 A),
invisible (p. 51 A), apprehended not by sense but by a bastard
kind of reason (p. 52 B), indestructible (*ib.*), and unchanging
(p. 50 B), receiving all things, but never itself assuming the

---

[1] Pp. 48 E-53 D.

[2] ἐν μὲν ὡς παραδείγματος εἶδος ὑπο-
τεθέν, νοητὸν καὶ ἀεὶ κατὰ ταὐτὰ ὄν,
μίμημα δὲ παραδείγματος δεύτερον, γένεσιν ἔχον καὶ ὁρατόν pp. 48 E-49 A.

[3] V. Bonitz Ind. *Arist.* p. 798 A.

[4] It is πάσης γενέσεως ὑποδοχή, οἷον
τιθήνη p. 49 A, ἡ τὰ πάντα δεχομένη
σώματα φύσις p. 50 B, it is an ἐκμαγεῖον
p. 50 C, ἡ τοῦ γεγονότος ὁρατοῦ καὶ πάντως

αἰσθητοῦ μήτηρ καὶ ὑποδοχή p. 51 A,
ἀνόρατον εἶδός τι καὶ ἄμορφον, πανδεχές,
μεταλάμβανον δὲ ἀπορώτατά πη τοῦ
νοητοῦ καὶ δυσαλωτότατον p. 51 A, B, τὸ
τῆς χώρας ἀεί, φθορὰν οὐ προσδεχόμενον,
ἕδραν δὲ παρέχον ὅσα ἔχει γένεσιν
πᾶσιν, αὐτὸ δὲ μετ' ἀναισθησίας ἁπτὸν
λογισμῷ τινι νόθῳ, μόγις πιστόν p. 52 A,
B, again in p. 52 D it is described briefly
as χώρα.

shape of any of the things it admits (p. 50 B, C, *cf.* D, E, p. 51 A), but supplying the room or space in which all processes of generation or becoming go on (p. 52 B), though it is itself distinct from this generation γένεσις (p. 52 D).

Now for the other two γένη; first, there is the ἐν ὡς παραδείγματος εἶδος ὑποτεθὲν νοητὸν καὶ ἀεὶ κατὰ ταὐτὰ ὄν p. 48 E. This is of course identical, as Plato himself intimates, with the Model spoken of in the early part of the dialogue. Secondly, there is the copy (μίμημα, p. 48 E, cp. pp. 50 C, 51 B) of the Model, which copy is identical with the sensible universe. This appears from (amongst other passages) p. 50 C χρὴ γένη διανοηθῆναι τριττά, τὸ μὲν γιγνόμενον (sensible things), τὸ δ' ἐν ᾧ γίγνεται (the substrate), τὸ δ' ὅθεν ἀφομοιούμενον φύεται τὸ γιγνόμενον. Now this substrate admits forms (ἰδέαι p. 50 D) of all kinds of things, and thus presents the appearance of fire, water, earth, and air (p. 51 B), these appearances being of course the γιγνόμενα (or γένεσις as they are called collectively, p. 52 D). But these forms of fire, water, earth, and air, which are thus presented to us, are only imitations, μιμήματα, of fire, etc., p. 51 B; there is a real Fire, etc., quite apart from the sensible " imitation " of fire, etc. These realities are absolute Ideas, grasped not by sense but by reason, καθ' αὐτὰ ἀναίσθητα ὑφ' ἡμῶν εἴδη, νοούμενα μόνον. Thus the Ideas are the models whose forms (*i.e.* copies of whose forms) are impressed on the substrate. It is these impressed forms which constitute the only objects of sense; the Ideas which are their Models are apprehended only by reason (p. 52 A), and the substrate by a bastard kind of reason (p. 52 B).

Thus the examination of this passage has proved that the Model spoken of in the early part of the dialogue was an Idea. The only doubt is as to the relation of that Idea to the other Ideas. The Model was (as we saw from p. 30 C) the Ideal Animal, and the universe was planned after this model. In the present passage the sensible universe would seem to contain the forms, not of one Idea only, but of a great number. These apparent discrepancies may perhaps be reconciled by supposing that the Idea of Animal includes in itself the Ideas of all other things, fire, earth, etc.

On the whole, the view taken of the Ideas in the *Timaeus*

is substantially the same as that which we find in the *Phaedo* and *Republic* ; they are the patterns to which sensible things bear an imperfect resemblance ; they are eternal, unchanging, and apprehended not by sense but by reason. The advance which is made in the *Timaeus* consists not so much in a modification of the Ideas themselves, as in the greater precision which is given to the conception of their sensible counterparts. Hitherto we have been told that sensible things partake in Ideas,[1] that they are the images [2] of the Ideas. But the question comes, what is it that partakes in the Ideas ? what is that on which the Images of the Ideas are cast ? If sensibles are modelled after the Ideas, what is that out of which they are modelled ? If sensibles get their form from the Ideas, whence do they get their matter ? The necessity of assuming some such material out of which the images are to be formed is admitted by Plato himself in that difficult sentence [3] of which the sense is rightly given by Stallbaum : " *Res sub sensus cadentes sunt illae quidem ad idearum exemplum compositae ideoque harum quasi imagines quaedam, sed tamen ab ipsis ideis diversae ; unde necesse est ut materiam aliquam habeant, in qua expressae sint, alioquin nihil omnino futurae* ". The answer then to these questions, Plato gives in the *Timaeus* by assuming this material substrate on which the Ideas impress their forms. It supplies the material out of which the copies are fashioned or at least the space in which they are fashioned. (For Plato seems to hesitate between regarding the ἀμυδρὸν εἶδος as " first matter " (to use an Aristotelian expression) or space. His illustrations, drawn from unguents and plastic substances, p. 50 E, and gold which can be moulded into all shapes, p. 50 A, B, point to the former view; his descriptions of it as χώρα, p. 52 D, and as ἕδραν παρέχον ὅσα ἔχει γένεσιν πᾶσιν, p. 52 B, make for the latter.)

There is a great likeness between the ἀμυδρὸν γένος and the ἄπειρον of the *Philebus*, and this is a point which deserves examination, for the *Timaeus* seems to form a sort of transition from the Ideal theory as it appears in the *Phaedrus*, *Phaedo*, and *Republic*, to the form which it assumes in the

---

[1] *Phaedo*, p. 102 B and C.   *Rep*. p. 520 C.
[2] εἰκόνες *Phaedr*. p. 250 B, εἴδωλα   [3] Pp. 52 C ὡς εἰκόνι μὲν κτλ.

Philebus (if indeed the Ideal theory appears in that dialogue at all, which seems doubtful). But not only does the substrate or Matter of the *Timaeus* bear a close resemblance to the ἄπειρον of the *Philebus*, but the Ideas of the *Timaeus* are similar (and, it seems to me, become more similar as the dialogue advances) to the πέρας of the *Philebus*. In other words, the theory on both sides (material and Ideal) approaches to those Pythagorean views which Plato held in later life, and of which he shows decided symptoms in the *Philebus*. I do not insist on the merely verbal argument that sensible things are described in the *Timaeus* [1] by that very term which Aristotle tells us was the only point which distinguished the Pythagorean from the Platonic theory— the word imitation.[2] A much more serious approximation, than a merely verbal one, to the system of Pythagoras can be shown to exist in the *Timaeus*. The sensible fire, air, water, and earth are modelled after the ideas of fire, air, water, and earth ; [3] this is pure Idealism. But what are fire, air, water, and earth ? They are (we are told) mathematical entities ; fire is a tetrahedron, air an octohedron, water an eikosihedron, earth a cube.[4] And what are the tetrahedron, etc. ? They are compounds of two triangles, one the right-angled isosceles, the other the right-angled scalene.[5] Thus we find that the sensible elements are modelled on Ideas, and that these Ideas [6] are ultimately reducible to a couple of triangles. If this is not Pythagoreanism, it is but one remove from it ; for whereas Plato here derives sensible things from geometrical notions, the Pythagoreans derived them from numbers, which are but one degree more abstract than geometrical notions. This very doctrine of fire being a tetrahedron, etc., is said by Zeller [7] to be a doctrine of Philolaus, and Philolaus, he tells us,[8] " macht den Versuch, theils das

---

[1] μίμημα δὲ παραδείγματος pp. 48 E-49 A, μιμήματα τούτων p. 51 B, τῶν ὄντων ἀεὶ ὄντα μιμήματα p. 50 C.

[2] οἱ μὲν γὰρ Πυθαγόρειοι μιμήσει τὰ ὄντα φασὶν εἶναι τῶν ἀριθμῶν, Πλάτων δὲ μεθέξει, τοὔνομα μεταβαλών Arist. *Metaph.* A p. 988 a 11-13.

[3] Pp. 51 B-52 A.

[4] *Tim.* pp. 55 D-56 B.

[5] P. 53 C, D.

[6] It might be objected that it is the sensible, not the Ideal, fire, air, etc., which are so reducible. But if the sensible fire, etc., are modelled on the Ideas, and the sensible are composed of triangles, surely the Ideas of fire, etc., must in like manner be reducible to Ideas of triangles.

[7] *Plato*, p. 372, Eng. tr.

[8] Vol. i. pp. 350-351.

Körperliche überhaupt, theils die physikalischen Grund-
eigenschaften der Körper aus den Figuren, und die Figuren
aus den Zahlen abzuleiten", so that Philolaus made
that last abstraction which Plato in the *Timaeus* stops
short of making — the derivation of the triangles from
numbers. Thus we understand what is meant when Plato says
καὶ τὸ μὲν δὴ πρὸ τούτου πάντα ταῦτ᾽ ἔχειν ἀλόγως καὶ
ἀμέτρως· ὅτε δ᾽ ἐπεχειρεῖτο κοσμεῖσθαι τὸ πᾶν, πῦρ πρῶτον
καὶ ὕδωρ καὶ γῆν καὶ ἀέρα, ἴχνη μὲν ἔχοντα αὐτῶν ἄττα,
παντάπασί γε μὴν διακείμενα ὥσπερ εἰκὸς ἔχειν ἅπαν ὅταν
ἀπῇ τινὸς θεός, οὕτω δὴ τότε πεφυκότα ταῦτα πρῶτον
διεσχημάτιστο εἴδεσί τε καὶ ἀριθμοῖς p. 53 A, B.   It would be wrong
to strain the last words too far ; they only mean that God
turned the previous chaos into a cosmos by introducing
forms and mathematical proportions ; still the juxtaposi-
tion of the watchwords of Pythagoreanism and Platonism
(ἀριθμοί—εἴδη), just at the point where the two systems are
about to meet, is curious.[1]

Hence the amount of mathematics in the *Timaeus*, *e.g.*
the mathematical proportions between fire, air, water, and
earth,[2] the mathematical composition of the soul of the world,[3]
the perfect number of time,[4] and the importance assigned to
the knowledge of numbers.[5]

Thus the Ideas, if not yet numbers, are on a fair way
to become so.   I have said that the ἀμυδρὸν γένος of the
Timaeus corresponds to the ἄπειρον of the *Philebus*.   Now
the πέρας of the *Philebus* is ὅ τί περ ἂν πρὸς ἀριθμὸν ἀριθμὸς
ἢ μέτρον ᾖ πρὸς μέτρον; and the Ideas in the *Timaeus*
certainly approach such a conception.   Moreover, the δημιουργός of the *Timaeus* is not far removed from the νοῦς of
the *Philebus*.[6]   Hence I consider that I am justified in hold-
ing that the Ideal theory in the *Timaeus* resembles (both on
the Material and Ideal side) the metaphysical theory of the

---

[1] With the above passage compare
a similar one, p. 69 B ταῦτα ἀτάκτως
ἔχοντα ὁ θεὸς ἐν ἑκάστῳ τε αὐτῷ πρὸς
αὐτὸ καὶ πρὸς ἄλληλα συμμετρίας ἐν-
εποίησεν, ὅσας τε καὶ ὅπῃ δυνατὸν ἦν
ἀνάλογα καὶ σύμμετρα εἶναι.
[2] Pp. 31 B-32 C.

[3] P. 35 B-D.
[4] P. 39 D.
[5] P. 47 A, B, C.
[6] Cp. *Phil.* pp. 28 C-30 E with such
passages as *Tim.* p. 69 B quoted just
above.

Philebus, that the *Timaeus* is in fact a transition from Idealism to Pythagoreanism.

Before concluding this hasty review of the *Timaeus* (so far as it bears on the Ideal theory), there are some points which remain to be noticed. One is that the Ideas are not represented either as the creation or the thoughts of God. They are simply represented as the Models which God looked to when He fashioned the sensible universe,[1] and as existing eternally.[2] Thus they appear, for all that is said about them, to be co-eternal with God. As for the identification of the cause of the creation (or rather ordering, for there existed a sort of chaos before)[3] of the world with God, we cannot be certain how far this is serious and how far (if at all) mythical, for Plato avoids an inquiry into this great cause; "to discover", he says, "the maker and father of this universe is hard, and even when we have discovered [him or it] it is impossible to explain [him or it] to all men".[4] With this remark he dismisses the question, and passes on, using that expression δ' οὖν by which a Greek indicated a transition from the uncertain or obscure to the certain or clear.

I have tried to show that in the tenth book of the *Republic* Ideas of concrete things appear for the first time. Here, in the *Timaeus*, we have Ideas of Fire καὶ πάντα περὶ ὧν ἀεὶ λέγομεν οὕτως αὐτὰ καθ' αὑτὰ ὄντα ἕκαστα p. 51 B. But we have already seen how soon these substances vanish into the thin air of mathematics.

Again the view that Plato never assumed Ideas of evil receives some support from the *Timaeus*. God is said in the creation of the world to have wished to make everything good and nothing evil,[5] and again after fashioning the immortal souls of men, He informs them of their destiny, the possibilities of good and evil, happiness and woe, ἵνα [αὐτὸς ὁ θεὸς] τῆς ἔπειτα εἴη κακίας ἑκάστων ἀναίτιος ; and after so doing, He left it to the created Gods to fashion the body and the mortal soul, and to guide man for the best, ὅτι μὴ κακῶν αὐτὸ ἑαυτῷ γίγνοιτο αἴτιον [scil. τὸ θνητὸν ζῷον], p. 42 E.[6]

---

[1] Pp. 28 E-29 A.
[2] Cp. especially c. x. pp. 37 C-38 B.
[3] Cp. pp. 30 A, 52 D-53 B, 69 B.
[4] P. 28 C, quoted above, p. 107.

[5] P. 30 A, this agrees with *Rep.* p. 379.
[6] Cp. *Rep.* x. p. 617 E αἰτία ἑλομένου· θεὸς ἀναίτιος.

In the passage last referred to (c. xiv. pp. 41 D *sqq.*) we have the last glimpse in Plato of the beautiful theory of "reminiscence". God is there said, after having created the immortal souls of men (*i.e.* the rational part, which alone is represented as immortal in the *Timaeus*, cp. c. 31), to have made them equal in number to the stars, then to have set them each in his starry chariot (ἐμβιβάσας ὡς εἰς ὄχημα p. 41 E) and shown them all the universe (τὴν του παντὸς φύσιν), and told them all the laws of fate, how they would first all be born alike into human form, but might afterwards through sin fall and pass into the form of beasts (after that of women, p. 42 B, cp. p. 90 E). This antenatal knowledge and the transmigration of souls are the same doctrines which we find in the *Phaedrus* and *Phaedo*, and the latter (transmigration) occurs also in the *Republic*. The parallel in Wordsworth to the Platonic doctrine of reminiscence is well known. " Our birth is but a sleep and a forgetting," etc. The two doctrines differ, however, and Plato's is the more manly and hopeful of the two, for while Wordsworth declares that the memory of " that imperial palace whence he came " is strongest in childhood and dies away altogether in manhood, Plato held that it was but faint in childhood but brightened as life went on. Wordsworth's is a theory of forgetfulness, Plato's of reminiscence ; the former would have us look back with regret to the past, the latter forward with hope to the future.

Lastly, I may, by the way, notice one more item in the debt which Aristotle owes to Plato. One of the most beautiful of Aristotle's sayings is almost a verbal copy of a passage in the *Timaeus*. Arist. *Nic. Eth.* p. 1177 b 33 *sqq.* οὐ χρὴ δὲ κατὰ τοὺς παραινοῦντας ἀνθρώπινα φρονεῖν ἄνθρωπον ὄντα οὐδὲ θνητὰ τὸν θνητόν, ἀλλ᾽ ἐφ᾽ ὅσον ἐνδέχεται ἀθανατίζειν καὶ πάντα ποιεῖν πρὸς τὸ ζῆν κατὰ τὸ κράτιστον τῶν ἐν αὐτῷ. With this compare Plato, *Timaeus*, p. 90 B, C τῷ δὲ περὶ φιλομαθίαν καὶ περὶ τὰς ἀληθεῖς φρονήσεις ἐσπουδακότι καὶ ταῦτα μάλιστα τῶν αὐτοῦ γεγυμνασμένῳ φρονεῖν μὲν ἀθάνατα καὶ θεῖα, ἄνπερ ἀληθείας ἐφάπτηται, πᾶσα ἀνάγκη που, καθ᾽ ὅσον δ᾽ αὖ μετασχεῖν ἀνθρωπίνη φύσις ἀθανασίας ἐνδέχεται, τούτου μηδὲν μέρος ἀπολείπειν, ἅτε δὲ ἀεὶ θεραπεύοντα τὸ θεῖον ἔχοντά τε αὐτὸν εὖ κεκοσμημένον τὸν δαίμονα ξύνοικον ἐν αὐτῷ διαφερόντως εὐδαίμονα εἶναι. The parallel seems to have escaped the commentators, if I may judge from Stallbaum on Plato and Grant on Aristotle.

XI

The *Parmenides* [1] consists of two main parts ; the first contains a brief exposition followed by a searching criticism of the Ideal theory ; the second consists of a long series of dialectical deductions from the proposition the One is. This latter part I shall not discuss, as I have not studied it sufficiently (having read it only once and that some years ago) to be able to pronounce an opinion upon it. Grote (like Strümpell, quoted by Grote, ii. p. 279 note) " sees no other purpose in these demonstrations than that of dialectical exercise ", and in this view I formerly concurred, but a better acquaintance with Plato leads me now to doubt seriously of its truth. The Germans extract various positive dogmas from the antinomies. I shall confine myself to the first part of the dialogue, the exposition and criticism of the Ideal theory.

The disputants are Zeno, Parmenides, and Socrates, the last of whom is represented as a youth. Zeno, in a written essay which he reads aloud, defends the doctrine of Parmenides that the One is, by exposing the contradictions which follow from the supposition that the Many are. If the Many are, they must be both like and unlike, which is impossible ; the unlike cannot be like, nor the like unlike. On this point the youthful Socrates joins issue with him, distinguishing particular things from their corresponding Ideas. There is (he holds [2]) an Idea of Likeness and an Idea of Unlikeness ; like things are like by partaking in the Idea of Likeness ; unlike things are unlike by partaking in the Idea of Unlikeness. Now things may quite well partake in both Ideas (that of Likeness and that of Unlikeness) at the same time, and thus may be at once like and unlike. From this it would follow (though this is not distinctly stated) that Zeno's proof of the non-existence of the Many is valueless, since it

---

[1] In my remarks on the *Philebus* I have tried to show some grounds for the order in which I have assumed the later dialogues to succeed each other.
[2] Pp. 128 E *sqq.*

is quite possible that the Many may partake of contrary qualities. But while things may partake of contrary qualities, the Ideas cannot. The Idea of Likeness can never partake of the Idea of Unlikeness, nor the latter of the former. Similarly things may be at the same time one by partaking in the Idea of One, and many by partaking in the Idea of Plurality. But the Idea of One can never be plural, nor the Idea of Plurality One. So with rest and motion, their Ideas can never partake of each other (p. 129 E).

[This incommunicability of the Ideas with each other is to be particularly observed, since it is noticed and refuted in the *Sophist*. This mutual exclusion of the Ideas has already appeared as a feature of the theory in the *Phaedo*,[1] and in the *Timaeus*.[2] Yet the way in which Socrates in the *Parmenides* rejects the notion of the communion of the Ideas is to be noticed. He does not directly deny the possibility of the thing ; he says that if anyone could prove the participation in each other of the Ideas of Like and Unlike, it would be extraordinary ;[3] again, if anyone could do the same with the Ideas of One and Many, he would be surprised ;[4] again, if any one proved that the Ideas (γένη τε καὶ εἴδη) partook of their opposites, it would be wonderful (ἄξιον θαυμάζειν, *ib.*) ; again, if any one could show that the Ideas (such as Like and Unlike, Many and One, Rest and Motion) could be united as well as separated, Socrates would be wonderfully surprised.[5]

I cannot help thinking that the writer of the dialogue intended thus to emphasize the paradoxical nature of the propositions he intended to prove, whether these proofs be discovered in the antinomies of the *Parmenides*, or, as is quite possible, in the *Sophist*.]

At this point Parmenides joins in the dialogue which had previously been conducted between Socrates and Zeno. He asks Socrates whether he assumes Ideas of justice, beauty, and goodness, and is answered in the affirmative.

---

[1] P. 102 D αὐτὸ τὸ μέγεθος οὐδέποτ' ἐθέλειν ἅμα μέγα καὶ σμικρὸν εἶναι.

[2] Pp. 51 E-52 A ὁμολογητέον ἐν μὲν εἶναι τὸ κατὰ ταῦτα [ταὐτὰ ?] ἔχον εἶδος, ἀγέννητον καὶ ἀνώλεθρον οὔτε εἰς ἑαυτὸ εἰς δεχόμενον ἄλλο ἄλλοθεν οὔτε αὐτὸ

εἰς ἄλλο ποι ἰόν.

[3] τέρας ἄν, οἶμαι, ἦν p. 129 B.

[4] τοῦτο ἤδη θαυμάσομαι p. 129 C.

[5] ἀγαίμην ἂν ἔγωγ', ἔφη, θαυμαστῶς p. 120 E.

Parmenides then inquires whether he admits ideas of man, fire, and water. Socrates replies that he has often hesitated whether he ought to do so or not ; but upon being further asked whether there are Ideas of Hair, Mud, and Dirt, he answers emphatically no. " The hair, mud, and dirt which we see are the only hair, mud, and dirt that exist ; to assume ideas of them would be absurd." Yet Socrates acknowledges that a doubt has often occurred to him whether it might not be true of all things [viz. that they have corresponding ideas], but he had always banished the thought, seeing the abyss of absurdity to which it led.

[I have already made use of this passage to show that Plato hesitated whether to assume ideas of substances or not. Even of such things as man, fire, and water, it is not asserted that there were Ideas—the point is left doubtful ; while there is (at first at least) no doubt at all (οὐδαμῶς *scil.* ἀπορῶ p. 130 D) that of hair, mud, and dirt there are no ideas. Zeller, who affirms [1] that Plato recognizes ideas of these latter things, seems to have misunderstood the passage. If we except the *Timaeus*, where the Ideas are so soon resolved into mathematical abstractions, there is only one place in Plato (*Republic* x.) where Ideas of concrete things are undoubtedly assumed.]

Parmenides then produces the following objections to the Ideal theory.

1. If particular things participate in Ideas, either the whole Idea or a part of it must be in each particular thing. Neither supposition is possible. For (*a*) if the whole Idea were in each thing, the same Idea would be in many separate things at the same time ; which is absurd. (*b*) If a part only of the Idea is in each thing, we make the Ideas divisible, and many absurd consequences follow. *E.g.* how can the Idea of Unity be divisible, and still be a unity ? Again it would follow that a great thing is great by reason of a part which is smaller than Greatness itself ; an equal thing will be equal by reason of a part which is less than Equality ; the Idea of Smallness will be greater than its part (since the whole is greater than its part) ; thus the Idea of *Small-ness* will be *greater* than something, and that to which a

[1] P. 273, Eng. tr.

part of Smallness is added will be made smaller by the addition.

Thus the particulars cannot participate in Ideas either as wholes or as parts ; but there is no other way in which they can participate in them : therefore they cannot participate in them at all.[1]

2. When you look (continues Parmenides) at a number of great things, you get a general notion of greatness the same for all, and it is this that makes you believe in an Idea of Greatness. But when you mentally contemplate the Idea of Greatness and all the particular great things, you get another Idea of Greatness, common both to the Idea and to the particulars ; thus you get a second Idea of Greatness over and above the first Idea of Greatness and the great particulars ; and by a similar process you will get a third Idea of Greatness, and so on to infinity, so that each idea will be not one, but infinite in number.[2]

3. Perhaps, says Socrates, the Idea is only a thought or conception (νόημα), and so can exist only in the soul. Parmenides points out that a conception must be a conception of something, some one existing thing which is conceived of as the same in all cases. But this thing conceived of as one, as always existent the same in all, must be the Idea. Again, if Ideas are conceptions and all things partake in Ideas, either all things consist of Ideas and therefore conceive, or are conceptions without the power of conceiving ; both suppositions are absurd.[3]

4. Socrates tries again. The Ideas (he says) are fixed models in nature. All other things are copies of, and like to, the Ideas. In saying that particulars *participate* in Ideas, we simply mean that particulars are *like* Ideas. In that case, replies Parmenides, the Ideas also must be like the particulars. But things are like each other only in so far as they partake in the Idea of Likeness. Therefore, particular like things and the Idea of Likeness must be like each other by partaking in a second Idea of Likeness ; and this process must go on to infinity. But this is impossible. Therefore the participation of things in Ideas cannot consist in a likeness to the Ideas.

[1] Pp. 130 E-131 E.   [3] P. 132 B, C.
[2] Pp. 131 E-132 B.

5. Parmenides next shows that on Socrates' own hypothesis the Ideas must be unknown to us. The Ideas are absolute, they exist by themselves, not in us. Now relative Ideas must be related to Ideas, not to particulars ; *e.g.* the Idea of Master must be related to the Idea of Servant, not to a particular servant. Similarly, relative things or particulars must be related to things, not to Ideas. If I am a master, I must be master of a particular servant, not of the Idea of Servant ; if I am a servant, I must be servant of a particular master, not of the Idea of Master.

Now Knowledge is relative : the Idea of Knowledge in general is related to the Idea of Truth, and the Idea of each special knowledge is relative to the Idea of each special thing. On the other hand, our knowledge in general is relative to our truth, and each of our special knowledges is relative to some particular thing. The Ideas we have not. But the Ideas are known by the Idea of Knowledge which we have not got ; therefore, the Ideas are not known by us at all.

6. You say (continues Parmenides) that there is an Idea of Knowledge which is far more perfect than our Knowledge, an Idea of Beauty far more perfect than our Beauty, etc. This perfect Ideal Knowledge must be possessed, if by any one, by God. But we saw that Ideas are relative only to Ideas, things (particulars) are relative only to things. Therefore the Idea of Mastership cannot rule us, the Idea of Knowledge cannot know us nor the particulars amid which we live. Thus God, having the Ideas of Mastership and of Knowledge, can neither rule us nor know us and our human affairs, any more than we can rule Him by our particular rule (ἀρχή) or know Him by our particular knowledge.[1]

The acuteness and force of these objections have been admitted by modern interpreters, and I shall not dwell upon them. One thing seems clear, that this dialogue could not have been written by Plato in the early days of his favourite theory. I fully agree with Strümpell[2] that "the *Parmenides* was composed at a time of Plato's life when he had become sensible of the difficulties and contradictions attaching to his doctrine of self-existent Forms or Ideas, and when he was looking about for some way of extrication from them", and

---

[1] P. 134 C-E.   [2] *Ap.* Grote, ii. p. 279 note.

I incline to think that Plato attempted to meet these difficulties by those modifications in his theory which we discover
in the *Sophist* and *Philebus*. To these two dialogues I now
pass, taking the *Sophist* first, because the views expressed in
the *Philebus* on the Ideal theory (if that theory appears at all
in the *Philebus*) are, it seems to me, much further removed
from those of the *Phaedo*, *Republic*, etc., than are those of
the *Sophist*, and it is therefore probable that the *Sophist*
preceded the *Philebus*.

XII

The *Sophist* contains an important modification of the
Ideal theory, such as is not to be found in any of the other
dialogues. This modification is in brief the κοινωνία τῶν
γενῶν or τῶν εἰδῶν.[1] This κοινωνία τῶν εἰδῶν has been
(it seems to me) misunderstood. It has been thought
(apparently by Mr. Grote, who says, ii. p. 460, " it is this
implication and conjunction of the Universal with its particulars which is the doctrine of the *Sophist* ") that this
κοινωνία is nothing but the participation of sensibles in
Ideas, that μέθεξις τῶν εἰδῶν,[2] which has been inculcated
over and over again in previous dialogues, and which
Aristotle thought was nonsense.[3] About this participation
of sensibles in Ideas I do not find one word in the dialogue.
The κοινωνία τῶν γενῶν in the *Sophist* is the participation
of Ideas *in each other*, and it is just this which is the novel
feature in the theory. The old μέθεξις of sensibles in Ideas
(to say nothing of being by this time somewhat stale) had
been pretty well knocked on the head by Parmenides,[4] and
never recovered sufficiently to take its place again in Plato ;
a faint sign of returning vitality is met by a flourish of the
Parmenidean cudgel.[5] A mere glance at the dialogue seems
to show that the " communion " spoken of is that of Ideas
in each other. The passage which discusses the κοινωνία
lasts from pp. 251 D to 259 E. The Stranger begins by asking

---

[1] For the phrase cp. *Soph.* pp. 254
B, C, 257 A, etc.

[2] The word μέθεξις does occur in
this dialogue (pp. 256 A, 259 A) with its
verb μετέχειν (*e.g.* pp. 251 E, 254 B,

D, E), but in the same sense as κοινωνία
and κοινωνεῖν.

[3] *Metaph.* A c. 9, p. 991 a 20-22.

[4] See above, pp. 91 *sq.*

[5] *Phileb.* p. 15 A, B.

whether the Ideas of rest, motion, etc., are all exclusive of each other, unable to participate in each other (μεταλαμβάνειν ἀλλήλων), or whether all are able to participate in each other (ἐπικοινωνεῖν ἀλλήλοις), or lastly whether some participate in each other and some do not. He shows the first two suppositions to be untenable, and accordingly adopts the last (p. 253 E). Thus it is the participation of the Ideas (γένη or εἴδη, the words are used as synonymous throughout the dialogue, cp. e.g. p. 254 B, C, D) in each other which is discussed, not the participation of sensibles in Ideas. The question is not, do moving things participate in the Idea of Motion, things at rest in the Idea of Rest, etc.? but, do the Ideas of Motion, Rest, etc., participate in each other?[1] The Ideas whose communion with each other Plato here determines are those of Being, Rest, Motion, Sameness, and Otherness. He does not profess to examine all the Ideas,[2] only the chief. Motion is (1) different from Rest, and therefore is not rest; yet motion is because it partakes of Being; (2) motion is different from the Same, and therefore is not the same; yet motion is the same with itself; (3) motion is different from Other, and therefore is not Other, yet motion is other (because it is other than rest, etc.); (4) motion is different from Being, and therefore is not Being, and yet it is, because it partakes in Being. Much the same might be shown of other Ideas. They (at least many of them) participate in each other: further, they all are not in so far as they are not identical with Being, yet they all are because they partake of Being. Thus in each Idea the quantity of Being contained is large, but the quantity of not being is infinite.[3] This Not-Being is simply a particular part of the general idea Other.[4]

---

[1] Compare p. 253 D τὰ γένη πρὸς ἄλληλα κατὰ ταὐτὰ μίξεως ἔχειν ὡμολογήκαμεν—ποῖα ποίοις συμφωνεῖ τῶν γενῶν καὶ ποῖα ἄλληλα οὐ δέχεται, p. 254 B τὰ μὲν ἡμῖν τῶν γενῶν ὡμολόγηται κοινωνεῖν ἐθέλειν ἀλλήλοις, ib. C μὴ περὶ πάντων τῶν εἰδῶν— κοινωνίας ἀλλήλων πῶς ἔχει δυνάμεως, p. 256 B τῶν γενῶν συγχωρησόμεθα τὰ μὲν ἀλλήλοις ἐθέλειν μίγνυσθαι τὰ δὲ μή, p. 257 A ἔχει κοινωνίαν ἀλλήλοις ἡ

τῶν γενῶν φύσις, p. 259 A συμμίγνυταί τε ἀλλήλοις τὰ γένη, ib. E τὴν ἀλλήλων τῶν εἰδῶν συμπλοκήν.

[2] σκοποῦντες μὴ περὶ πάντων τῶν εἰδῶν, ἵνα μὴ ταραττώμεθα ἐν πολλοῖς p. 254 C.

[3] P. 256 E περὶ ἕκαστον ἄρα τῶν εἰδῶν πολὺ μέν ἐστι τὸ ὄν, ἄπειρον δὲ πλήθει τὸ μὴ ὄν.

[4] τὴν γὰρ θατέρου φύσιν ἀποδείξαντες οὖσάν τε καὶ κατακεκερματισμένην ἐπὶ

This is new with a vengeance. Hitherto the Ideas have stood alone in solitary grandeur, stars that " dwelt apart ".[1] It was the characteristic of the Ideas that each was absolute, αὐτὸ καθ' αὐτό. Now in the *Sophist* they are found to participate in each other. And not only do Ideas partake in their opposites (the possibility of which was so positively denied in the *Phaedo* [2]), e.g. Idea of Same in Idea of Other, but, moreover, each idea, along with a share of Being (which they and they alone have always had according to the Ideal theory) has also (*horrible dictu !*) a share of Not-Being, and, what is more, a great deal more of it than of Being.[3] Alas ! and has it come to this ? How are the mighty fallen ! The very essence of sensible things was that they were compounded of Being and Not-Being (*Republic* v.) ; and if Ideas can be shown to be similar compounds, then good-bye to the Ideas. For Plato's chief reason for distinguishing the sensible from the Ideal world was that sensible things admit of contrary predicates, while ideas never do,[4] but if it appears that the Ideas also admit of such contrary predicates, all reason for drawing a distinction between the two worlds has vanished.

But, hark, the sound of voices in earnest altercation. Let us draw near and listen. The Stranger is remonstrating with some one unseen, and a voice replies, "Far up the height ". What is the voice saying ? " νοητὰ ἄττα καὶ ἀσώματα εἴδη τὴν ἀληθινὴν οὐσίαν εἶναι, τὰ δὲ ἐκείνων σώματα καὶ τὴν λεγομένην ὑπ' αὐτῶν ἀλήθειαν γένεσιν ἀντ' οὐσίας

πάντα τὰ ὄντα πρὸς ἄλληλα, τὸ πρὸς ὃν ἕκαστον μόριον αὐτῆς ἀντιτιθέμενον ἐτολμήσαμεν εἰπεῖν ὡς αὐτὸ τοῦτό ἐστιν ὄντως τὸ μὴ ὄν p. 258 D, E, cp. p. 275 D κατὰ πάντα γὰρ ἡ θατέρου φύσις ἕτερον ἀπεργαζομένη τοῦ ὄντος ἕκαστον οὐκ ὂν ποιεῖ.

[1] Cp. *Timaeus*, p. 52 A τὸ κατὰ ταὐτὰ ἔχον εἶδος, ἀγέννητον καὶ ἀνώλεθρον, οὔτε εἰς ἑαυτὸ εἰσδεχόμενον ἄλλο ἄλλοθεν οὔτε αὐτὸ εἰς ἄλλο ποι ἰόν. *Parmen.* p. 129 B εἰ μὲν γὰρ αὐτὰ τὰ ὅμοιά τις ἀπέφαινεν ἀνόμοια γιγνόμενα, ἢ τὰ ἀνόμοια ὅμοια, τέρας ἄν, οἶμαι, ἦν, ib. C εἰ μὲν αὐτὰ τὰ γένη τε καὶ εἴδη ἐν αὐτοῖς ἀποφαίνοι τἀναντία ταῦτα πάθη

πάσχοντα, ἄξιον θαυμάζειν, ib. D and E ἐὰν δέ τις ὃ νῦν δὴ ἐγὼ ἔλεγον, πρῶτον μὲν διαιρῆται χωρὶς αὐτὰ καθ' αὐτὰ τὰ εἴδη, οἷον ὁμοιότητά τε καὶ ἀνομοιότητα καὶ πλῆθος καὶ τὸ ἓν καὶ στάσιν καὶ κίνησιν καὶ πάντα τὰ τοιαῦτα, εἶτα ἐν ἑαυτοῖς ταῦτα δυνάμενα συγκεράννυσθαι καὶ διακρίνεσθαι ἀποφαίνῃ, ἀγαίμην ἂν ἔγωγ', ἔφη, θαυμαστῶς, *Phaedo*, p. 103 B αὐτὸ τὸ ἐναντίον ἑαυτῷ ἐναντίον οὐκ ἂν ποτε γένοιτο.

[2] cc. 50, 51.

[3] *Soph.* p. 256 E, quoted on preceding page.

[4] *Rep.* v. p. 479.

φερομένην τινά." The voice seems familiar; we have heard something like that before. But let us listen again. "σώματι μὲν ἡμᾶς γενέσει δι' αἰσθήσεως κοινωνεῖν, διὰ λογισμοῦ δὲ ψυχῇ πρὸς τὴν ὄντως οὐσίαν, ἢ ἀεὶ κατὰ ταὐτὰ ὡς αὐτῶς ἔχει, γένεσιν δὲ ἄλλοτε ἄλλως." Surely we can doubt no longer, " *aut Plato aut Diabolus* ". That in the cloud-walkers of the famous γιγαντομαχία (*Sophist*, p. 246 A, etc.) we are to recognize Plato himself, is not the usual opinion. That the whole description of these aerial philosophers down to the minutest particular applies to Plato, is certain ; that it applies to the Megarians, is an hypothesis. Yet the majority of critics appear to desert the certainty in order to embrace the hypothesis, and Zeller is so certain of its truth that he supplements our defective knowledge of Megarian doctrines by passages drawn from the *Sophist*. (There is a tempting round here for some critic to tread, though I am not aware that any one has availed himself of that mode of exercise in the present case. Certainly Zeller keeps the straight path.)

It seems almost wasting time to show by a comparison of passages that the Ideal doctrine described in the *Sophist* (*l.c.*) is identical with that of Plato himself in the *Phaedo, Republic,* etc. These ideal philosophers are φίλοι τῶν εἰδῶν p. 248 A ; they place reality in Ideas (τῶν ἐν εἴδεσιν αὐτὴν [*scil.* τὴν οὐσίαν] τιθεμένων p. 246 C) ; they insist that true being consists in Ideas which are intelligible and bodiless (νοητὰ ἄττα καὶ ἀσώματα εἴδη βιαζόμενοι τὴν ἀληθινὴν οὐσίαν εἶναι p. 246 B). Is it necessary to quote passages to prove that these were Plato's views. However, we may refer to *Republic*, pp. 507 B, C, 510 A, *Timaeus*, p. 52 A. Further, these Idealists break up sensible bodies by arguments (κατὰ σμικρὰ διαθραύοντες ἐν τοῖς λόγοις p. 246 C, D) and call sensible things γένεσις instead of οὐσία, and this γένεσις (they hold) is in motion (φερομένην τινά). I am almost ashamed to refer to such passages as *Republic*, p. 534 A, *Timaeus*, pp. 27 E-28 A, *ib.* p. 52 E, to prove that Plato distinguished the Ideal and sensible worlds as respectively ὄντα and γιγνόμενα, or (in the abstract) as οὐσία and γένεσις (the terms used in *Republic*, pp. 525 B, 527 E, 534 A). A specimen of the way of " breaking up sensible bodies by arguments " is given us in *Republic* v. p. 479. That sensible things are in constant motion is a doctrine of the

Theaetetus.   Further these Idealists held that with the body we, through the senses, hold communion with γένεσις, while with the soul we hold communion with ἡ ὄντως οὐσία, which is always the same (ἀεὶ κατὰ ταὐτὰ ὡσαύτως ἔχειν p. 248 A).[1] Further these philosophers sit on high in an unseen place.   With this compare the description of the true philosopher at the beginning of this dialogue οἱ μὴ πλαστῶς ἀλλ' ὄντως φιλόσοφοι, καθορῶντες ὑψόθεν τὸν τῶν κάτω βίον p. 216 C, and numerous allusions in the seventh book of the *Republic* to the elevated position of the philosopher of Ideas.[2]

Two points are to be particularly observed : firstly, these philosophers held that the εἴδη are known by the soul through reasoning, and so did Plato.   Secondly, they held that these Ideas are unchanging, ἀεὶ κατὰ ταὐτὰ ἔχοντα, and so did Plato.   Now the Eleatic stranger undertakes to show that these two doctrines (viz. (1) that the Ideas are unchanging, and (2) that they are known by reason) are inconsistent : that if the former is true, the latter is impossible ; if you hold

---

[1] Compare with this *Theaet.* pp. 184 B-187 A, particularly αὐτὴ δι' αὑτῆς ἡ ψυχὴ τὰ κοινά μοι φαίνεται περὶ πάντων ἐπισκοπεῖν, and again ἐν μὲν ἄρα τοῖς παθήμασιν οὐκ ἔνι ἐπιστήμη, ἐν δὲ τῷ περὶ ἐκείνων συλλογισμῷ· οὐσίας γὰρ καὶ ἀληθείας ἐνταῦθα μέν, ὡς ἔοικε, δυνατὸν ἅψασθαι, ἐκεῖ δὲ ἀδύνατον, but especially *Phaedo*, cc. 25, 26, 27, pp. 78 B-79 D, particularly αὐτὴ ἡ οὐσία —πότερον ὡσαύτως ἀεὶ ἔχει κατὰ ταὐτά, ἢ ἄλλοτ' ἄλλως ;—Ὡσαύτως, ἔφη, ἀνάγκη, ὁ Κέβης, κατὰ ταὐτὰ ἔχειν, ὦ Σώκρατες. Τί δὲ τῶν πολλῶν καλῶν οἷον ἀνθρώπων ἢ ἵππων ἢ ἱματίων ἢ ἄλλων ὡντινωνοῦν ἢ ἴσων ἢ καλῶν ἢ πάντων τῶν ἐκείνοις ὁμωνύμων; ἆρα κατὰ ταὐτὰ ἔχει, ἢ πᾶν τοὐναντίον ἐκείνοις οὔτε αὐτὰ αὑτοῖς οὔτε ἀλλήλοις οὐδέποτε, ὡς ἔπος εἰπεῖν, οὐδαμῶς κατὰ ταὐτά ἐστιν ; Οὕτως αὖ, ἔφη, ταῦτα, ὁ Κέβης· οὐδέποτε ὡσαύτως ἔχει. Οὐκοῦν τούτων μὲν κἂν ἅψαιο, κἂν ἴδοις, κἂν ταῖς ἄλλαις αἰσθήσεσιν αἴσθοιο, τῶν δὲ κατὰ ταὐτὰ ἐχόντων οὐκ ἔστιν ὅτῳ ποτ' ἂν ἄλλῳ ἐπιλάβοιο ἢ τῷ τῆς διανοίας λογισμῷ, ἀλλ' ἐστὶν ἀειδῆ τὰ τοιαῦτα καὶ οὐχ

ὁρᾶται (pp. 78 C-79 A). Also *ib.* p. 79 C, D ἡ ψυχή, ὅταν μὲν τῷ σώματι προσχρῆται εἰς τὸ σκοπεῖν τι ἢ διὰ τοῦ ὁρᾶν ἢ διὰ τοῦ ἀκούειν ἢ δι' ἄλλης τινὸς αἰσθήσεως—τοῦτο γάρ ἐστι τὸ διὰ τοῦ σώματος, τὸ δι' αἰσθήσεως σκοπεῖν τι— τότε μὲν ἕλκεται ὑπὸ τοῦ σώματος εἰς τὰ οὐδέποτε κατὰ ταὐτὰ ἔχοντα—ὅταν δέ γε αὐτὴ καθ' αὑτὴν σκοπῇ, ἐκεῖσε οἴχεται εἰς τὸ καθαρόν τε καὶ ἀεὶ ὂν καὶ ἀθάνατον καὶ ὡσαύτως ἔχον, καὶ ὡς συγγενὴς οὖσα αὐτοῦ ἀεὶ μετ' ἐκείνου τε γίγνεται, ὅτανπερ αὐτὴ καθ' αὑτὴν γένηται καὶ ἐξῇ αὐτῇ, καὶ πέπαυται τε τοῦ πλάνου καὶ περὶ ἐκεῖνα ἀεὶ κατὰ ταὐτὰ ὡσαύτως ἔχει, ἅτε τοιούτων ἐφαπτομένη.

[2] τὴν εἰς τὸν νοητὸν τόπον τῆς ψυχῆς ἄνοδον p. 517 B, ἀναβῆναι ἐκείνην τὴν ἀνάβασιν p. 519 D, ἀληθινὴν τοῦ ὄντος οὖσαν ἐπάνοδον p. 521 B, etc. Cp. too *Theaet.* p. 174 A, etc. When the lawyer is put perforce in the position of the philosopher, he is described as ἰλιγγιῶν τε ἀφ' ὑψηλοῦ κρεμασθεὶς καὶ βλέπων μετέωρος ἄνωθεν p. 175 D. Cp. *Phaedr.* p. 249.

the latter you must give up the former. Now this demonstration (p. 248), if it is good against the airy philosophers, is good just so far against Plato himself who held exactly these doctrines. Already in the *Parmenides* Plato saw that if the Ideas are absolute they cannot be known by us.[1] Now as there is no doubt that in the latter dialogue it is Plato's own ideal theory which is shown to make knowledge impossible, why should we in the *Sophist* go out of our way to suppose that the same theory which is met by the same objection is not Plato's but that of the Megarians?

In short, Plato realized in later life (as he indicates in the *Parmenides* and *Sophist*) that a knowledge of absolute, unchanging ideas is impossible for us. The theory broke down in two ways, both of which are brought into view in the *Sophist*. The absoluteness of the Ideas might be looked at from two points of view ; they were absolute in respect of us, and (if we except their subordination to the Good in the *Republic*) in respect of each other. Both of these absolutes (if I may say so) are shown in the *Sophist* to be incompatible with knowledge by us of the ideas. First, in relation to us : if the Ideas are to be known by us, they must stand in some relation to us, and this relation destroys their absoluteness.[2] Secondly, in relation to each other : if the Ideas are absolute in respect of each other, if they stand totally apart from each other, all true knowledge of them is impossible, for knowledge is a combination of notions, a judgement.[3] These two objections to the Ideal theory Plato meets in this dialogue by two distinct modifications of that theory. To meet the former objection he endows the Ideas with life, motion, and intelligence[4] (on the principle, perhaps, that like can only be known by like,[5] the principle which seems to have led Berkeley to suppose that all the objects perceived by our senses must be Ideas in the mind of God) : to meet the second, he makes the Ideas participate in each other.[6] Both these modifications of the Ideal theory are novelties ; never before were the Ideas

---

[1] *Parmen.* pp. 133 B-134 C, *supra*, 93.

[2] *Soph.* p. 248.

[3] Cp. *Soph.* p. 259 E τελεωτάτη πάντων λόγων ἐστὶν ἀφάνισις τὸ διαλύειν ἕκαστον ἀπὸ πάντων· διὰ γὰρ τὴν τῶν ἀλλήλων

τῶν εἰδῶν συμπλοκὴν ὁ λόγος γέγονεν ἡμῖν.

[4] Pp. 248 E-249 A.

[5] Cp. *Phaedo*, pp. 78 C-79 E, Aristot. *de Anima*, i. 2. § 7.

[6] Pp. 251-259 E.

represented as living and intelligent beings, never before were they represented as participating in each other. But in attempting to prop up the theory, Plato has really destroyed it, for by the former modification he did away with that un-changing nature which had previously distinguished Ideas from sensibles ; and by the latter he showed that Ideas resemble sensibles in admitting of contrary predicates, so that there no longer existed any need to distinguish an Ideal from the sensible world.

The fact is, there is no use mincing matters, the Ideal world has collapsed ; the sky has fallen and down tumble the Ideas, then pick themselves up and walk about trying to look as like ordinary beings as possible. They drop their titles of honour ; would you believe it, there is not an αὐτο- any-thing among them, they are plain Justice,[1] Motion, and so on. It is true that in an earlier part of the dialogue they still dwelt aloft, for we find the Eleatic stranger holloing to them, and their answer comes faintly back from the height.[2] They had been warned before by Parmenides to come down, and now the remorseless stranger lays the axe to the root of the tree, and it is all over with the Ideas. And we shall meet them no more in Plato. Half smilingly, half tearfully, we bid them farewell. So fade the dreams of youth.

By way of Appendix I may give a list of the Ideas men-tioned or hinted at in the *Sophist*.

Besides the leading Ideas of Being, Motion, Rest, Identity, and Difference, there are expressed, or apparently implied, ideas of Number, including Unity and Plurality (p. 238 A, B), of Justice and Injustice, Wisdom (φρόνησις) and Folly, and generally, of all the virtues and vices (τῆς ἄλλης ἀρετῆς καὶ τῶν ἐναντίων) (p. 247 A, B), of Beauty, Greatness, and Justice (pp. 257 E-258 A).

Here it will be observed that though there are no Ideas of sensible substances mentioned, there are apparently im-plied Ideas of vices. But in the first place, it is doubtful whether in the passage p. 247 A, B, Plato really refers to Ideas at all ; and secondly, at the time when he wrote the *Sophist*, the

[1] P. 247 A.   [2] P. 248.

metaphysical side of the Ideal theory (which was of course its characteristic side) was giving way to the logical, as we see in the discussion on the κοινωνία τῶν γενῶν. And logically, of course, there are general ideas of vices just as much as of virtues.

XIII

I have said that the Ideal theory appears no more in Plato. The only dialogue which might be quoted to disprove this remark is the *Philebus*. Upon the question whether or not the Ideal theory does appear here under the guise of the πέρας and ἄπειρον, I have at last decided to offer no opinion, for I am conscious that I do not sufficiently understand the dialogue to be able to form a definite opinion of its meaning. I shall therefore content myself with pointing out a few scattered facts, some of which seem to make for, others against, the theory that in the *Philebus* the Ideas are present in mufti.

But first a few words as to the order of the dialogues *Republic*, *Parmenides*, *Sophist*, and *Philebus*. I have taken these dialogues to follow each other in chronological order as I have named them. (The *Politicus* probably succeeded the *Sophist*, but with it I am not here concerned.[1]) Zeller [2] thinks these dialogues appeared thus : *Sophist*, *Parmenides*, *Philebus*, *Republic*. In placing the *Sophist* before the *Parmenides*, he seems to contradict implicitly an opinion which he has expressed elsewhere. In vol. i. pp. 509, 510 note (4th ed.), he holds that the meeting of Socrates and Parmenides in the dialogue *Parmenides* is fictitious, not historical. But in the *Sophist*, p. 218 E, there is an allusion to the meeting of Socrates and Parmenides. Now if this meeting was merely fictitious (as Zeller supposes it was), the allusion in the *Sophist* must be to the dialogue *Parmenides*, and the *Sophist* must therefore have been written later than the *Parmenides*. If Zeller admitted that the meeting was historical, then the allusion in the *Sophist* would prove nothing

[1] And probably the *Timaeus* soon followed the *Republic*. In saying that the *Republic, Parmenides, Sophist*, and *Philebus* succeeded each other in chronological order, I do not mean that no other dialogues appeared in the intervals between them.

[2] Eng. tr. p. 138.

as to the date of the dialogue relative to the dialogue *Parmenides*. Zeller has thus an alternative : if he holds that the meeting of Socrates and Parmenides is imaginary, he must give up the opinion that the *Sophist* is earlier than the *Parmenides* ; if he prefers to adhere to the latter opinion, he must acknowledge that the meeting was historical. He might perhaps reply that the allusion in the *Sophist* may be to an imaginary meeting of Socrates and Parmenides, and that still the *Sophist* might have preceded the *Parmenides*. But it is most improbable that Plato would have invented this meeting in such a passing and purposeless way, and the improbability is strengthened by the very similar allusion in the *Theaetetus*,[1] the bearing of which on the date of the latter dialogue I have briefly pointed out.[2] In short, no one, I think, will dispute the position, that the references in the *Theaetetus* and *Sophist* to a meeting between Socrates and Parmenides are allusions, either to an historical meeting between these philosophers, or to the dialogue *Parmenides*. If this be granted, Zeller has to choose between the horns of the dilemma which I have indicated. On the whole, I prefer to suppose that the meeting was imaginary, and accordingly, that the allusion in the *Sophist* to that meeting proves that the last mentioned dialogue was written later than the *Parmenides*.

Further, Zeller assumes that these two dialogues (*Parmenides* and *Sophist*), along with the *Philebus*, preceded the *Republic*. His grounds are that the *Parmenides* refers to the *Sophist*, that the *Philebus* refers to the *Parmenides*, and that the *Republic* refers to the *Philebus*. But that the *Republic* refers to, and was therefore written later than, the *Philebus* cannot be shown ; everything points the other way. The only argument which Zeller adduces (p. 138 *n.*) to prove the *Republic* later than the *Philebus* is the passage in *Republic* vi. p. 505 B ἀλλὰ μὴν τόδε γε οἶσθα ὅτι τοῖς μὲν πολλοῖς ἡδονὴ δοκεῖ εἶναι τὸ ἀγαθόν, τοῖς δὲ κομψοτέροις φρόνησις, κτλ. "When", says Zeller, "the question which forms the subject of the *Philebus* is thus discussed here as if it were a well-known one, and the two theories there criticized at length are dismissed with a few remarks, we cannot help

P. 183 E.   [2] P 20.

seeing here in the *Republic* a direct allusion to the *Philebus*."
This, it seems to me, is an excellent specimen of that bookish-
ness which cannot realize that there were in antiquity any
opinions besides those we find in books; so that an allusion
like that in the *Republic*, *l.c.*, must forsooth be a reference,
not to current views of the day, but to something which
Plato himself has written elsewhere. But the very terms in
which Plato makes the allusion surely show that he was referring to a current view of the day, not necessarily to anything he himself had written. (" You must know of course "
(τόδε γε οἶσθα) " that *the majority of men* think the good is
pleasure, and that the more refined think it is wisdom.")
But if the words in which Plato makes the allusion were not
sufficient to show that the views he alludes to were widely
spread, not merely men of straw set up in the schools to
be knocked down by the philosopher and his pupils, we
would have been convinced of the fact from history which
informs us that the views alluded to were actually held by
existing, contemporary sects, the Cynics and Cyrenaics
(though τοῖς πολλοῖς includes more than the Cyrenaics; it
intimates that the majority of men hold substantially Cyrenaic
views). In the face of the historical fact of the existence of
such contemporary schools, how can Zeller be certain that
in the *Republic* Plato is alluding, not to these current views,
but to his own discussion of them elsewhere? On a similar
principle a critic of some future age may assume that a passing allusion to the development theory by a writer of the
nineteenth century, who in another work discusses that theory
with greater fullness, must refer, not to a view which was
current in the writer's lifetime, but to what the writer himself
elsewhere states at greater length. When will critics shake
off the dust of their libraries, and remember that men do not
live in books alone?

The allusion, then, in the *Republic* to the two views about
the chief good proves nothing as to the date of the dialogue.
But a comparison of the contents of the *Republic* and *Philebus*
seems to prove that the *Republic* is the earlier of the two.
In the *Republic* we have, as I have tried to show, the Ideal
theory pure and simple, in its most developed form. It is
the natural consequent of the *Cratylus, Phaedrus, Sym-*

posium, and *Phaedo*. But the *Philebus* is very different; with its great principles of πέρας and ἄπειρον it is Pythagorean rather than Platonic, and we know that Pythagoreanism was a late feature in Plato's writings. How, then, any critic can break the series of purely Ideal dialogues by inserting among them one which is almost purely Pythagorean, I find it hard to understand.

The *Philebus*, then, is later than the *Republic*. So are the *Parmenides* and *Sophist*. For neither the objections urged in both dialogues against the Ideal theory nor the modifications of that theory contained in *Sophist* could (it seems to me) have been in Plato's mind when he wrote the *Republic*. Thus the *Parmenides*, *Sophist*, and *Philebus* are later than the *Republic*. It remains to determine the chronological order amongst the three dialogues themselves. First, the *Parmenides* must come before the *Sophist* (as I have tried to show by the allusion in *Sophist*, p. 217 C); moreover, it seems to have preceded the *Philebus*, for the latter dialogue with its Pythagorean colouring seems certainly later than the *Sophist*, which contains few or no traces of Pythagoreanism. Thus I conclude that the *Parmenides*, *Sophist*, and *Philebus* are all later than the *Republic*; that the *Sophist* alludes to, and is therefore later than, the *Parmenides*; that the *Philebus* is later than the *Sophist*, and therefore later than the *Parmenides*. Thus we get the order in which I have taken these dialogues : *Republic, Parmenides, Sophist, Philebus* (leaving out of view dialogues, such as the *Timaeus* and *Politicus*, which were probably written in some of the intervals between the publication of the four dialogues I have named).

[*Note.*—There are in the *Parmenides*, *Sophist*, and *Philebus* very similar passages on the popular difficulties about One and Many; viz. *Parmenides*, p. 129 B-D, *Sophist*, p. 251 A-C, *Philebus*, p. 14 C-E. But since these passages probably refer directly to the discussions of the day, and not to each other, nothing can be inferred from them as to the respective dates of the dialogues in which they occur.]

But to leave the question of the date, and turn to allusions to the Ideal theory which are to be found in the *Philebus* :

The first passage which concerns us is p. 14 C *sqq.*, which notices the vulgar difficulties about the One and Many. These difficulties arise (as he indicates) from the apparent opposition between the unity of a physical thing regarded as a whole, and the multiplicity of (*a*) its metaphysical and (*b*) its physical parts. (The difficulty with reference to the metaphysical parts is stated by Protarchus, p. 14 C, D, that with reference to the physical parts by Socrates, *ib.* D, E.) After putting aside these difficulties as childish (παιδαριώδη p. 14 D), Socrates states the difficulties of the one and many as they arise on the Ideal theory. These difficulties are nearly identical with the objections raised by Parmenides [1] to the Platonic theory of the participation of sensibles in Ideas. How can the Idea, which is always unchanging, be assumed to be in the changing particulars of sense ? Can these unchanging ideas be split into parts of which one appears in each particular of sense ? or can the Idea exist in its entirety in each particular sensible ? That would be absurd, for then the Idea would exist apart from itself. The solution of these difficulties, if it is given at all in the *Philebus*, is not obvious. Further, the very existence of the Ideas is stated as problematical.[2] Again, the Ideas are not mentioned by their names (εἴδη or ἰδέαι) at all. Instead of the αὐτὸς ἄνθρωπος, αὐτὸ καλόν, etc., we have εἶς ἄνθρωπος, ἓν καλόν, ἓν ἀγαθόν, etc. (p. 15 A), and in general they are ἕν (cp. p. 16 D τῶν ἓν ἐκείνων), ἑνάδες and μονάδες (p. 15 A, B). [If these monads are Ideas, then Ideas of sensible substances are mentioned, for we have ἕνα ἄνθρωπον and βοῦν ἕνα as well as τὸ καλὸν ἕν and τἀγαθὸν ἕν p. 15 A.] These names indicate a transition to the mathematical or Pythagorean way of regarding the Ideas. Later in the dialogue we have αὐτὴ δικαιοσύνη and αὐτὴ ἡ θεία σφαῖρα, and these expressions certainly point to Ideas. But though the words εἴδη and ἰδέαι occur,[3] they are never, I believe, used in their old technical sense. Perhaps the only apparent exception is p. 64 E εἰ μὴ μιᾷ δυνάμεθα ἰδέᾳ τὸ ἀγαθὸν θηρεῦσαι, but the very question shows that the ἰδέα is a form of thought, a formula, not a self-existing Idea.

The description of Dialectic and its province in pp. 57 E-59 D certainly reminds us of the old distinction between sensibles

---

[1] See above, pp. 91 *sq.*

[2] ἀμφισβήτησις γίγνεται—πρῶτον μὲν εἴ τινας δεῖ τοιαύτας εἶναι μονάδας ὑπο-

λαμβάνειν ἀληθῶς οὔσας.

[3] For ἰδέα cp. pp. 16 D, 25 B, 64 E; for εἶδος pp. 23 C and D, 33 C.

and Ideas. Thus the truest knowledge (ἀληθεστάτη γνῶσις) is said to have for its object τὸ ὂν καὶ τὸ ὄντως καὶ τὸ κατὰ ταὐτὸν ἀεὶ πεφυκός p. 58 A. Here too νοῦς and φρόνησις (pp. 58 D, 59 D) are distinguished from δόξα (p. 59 A) which, as of old, has for its object the sensible world, with its processes of change,[1] and this sensible world cannot be clearly known, since it never remains the same (p. 59 A, B). All this is quite in harmony with the old form of the Ideal theory. On the relation of the main theory of the dialogue (the four γένη, viz. the ἄπειρον, πέρας, μῖξις, and αἰτία) to the Ideal theory, I had intended offering a suggestion, but have decided to refrain from doing so, partly because the suggestion was fanciful, vague, and improbable, partly because the patience of the reader probably, and of the writer certainly, is wellnigh exhausted.

One more point about the *Philebus* and I have done. The prominence assigned to mind in the universe is notable. Mind or reason is said to have care of (ἐπιτροπεύειν), to arrange and guide the universe.[2] This mind is practically God (cp. p. 30 C, D) and the Creator of the universe (at least of the sensible universe), for all things are, it is said, a mixture of the Limit and Unlimited, and it is Mind which is the cause of this mixture.[3] The prominence thus assigned to Mind or God as the creative or at least regulative power of the universe is a feature which is found in none of the earlier Platonic writings, but in all the later dialogues (except the *Parmenides*) from the tenth book of the *Republic* downwards. [In the *Phaedo*, p. 97 B, etc., Plato would gladly have believed Mind was the cause of all things, but failed in his attempt to prove it.] Thus in *Republic* x. p. 597 B God is the Creator of the Ideas ; in the *Timaeus* throughout (as I have shown) God is described as the Creator (δημιουργός, ὁ γεννήσας πατήρ, etc.) ; so in the *Sophist*, c. 49, p. 265 B-E (ζῷα δὴ πάντα θνητὰ καὶ φυτά, ὅσα τ᾽ ἐπὶ γῆς ἐκ σπερμάτων καὶ

---

[1] Cp. p. 59 A οὐ περὶ τὰ ὄντα ἀεί, περὶ δὲ τὰ γιγνόμενα καὶ γενησόμενα καὶ γεγονότα.

[2] τὰ ξύμπαντα καὶ τόδε τὸ καλούμενον ὅλον, etc., *Phil.* pp. 28 D-30 E.

[3] This mixture is of course the sensible universe. It is variously designated as τὸ ἐξ ἀμφοῖν τούτοιν

[*scil.* the Limit and Unlimited] ἕν τι ξυμμισγόμενον p. 23 C, τὸ μικτὸν ἐκ τούτοιν ἀμφοῖν p. 25 B, τὸ τούτων ἔκγονον ἅπαν, γένεσιν εἰς οὐσίαν ἐκ τῶν μετὰ τοῦ πέρατος ἀπειργασμένων μέτρων p. 26 D, ἐκ τούτων τρίτον μικτὴν καὶ γεγενημένην οὐσίαν p. 27 B.

ῥιζῶν φύεται καὶ ὅσα ἄψυχα ἐν γῇ ξυνίσταται σώματα τηκτὰ καὶ ἄτηκτα, μῶν ἄλλον τινὸς ἢ θεοῦ δημιουργοῦντος φήσομεν ὕστερον γίγνεσθαι πρότερον οὐκ ὄντα;) ; so in *Politicus* God is described in relation to the universe as ὁ συναρμόσας, ὁ γεννήσας (p. 269 C, D) and as δημιουργός (p. 270 A); so in the present passage of the *Philebus* (pp. 29 D-30 E); and so in *Laws*, Book X.

(ψυχήν, ὦ ἑταῖρε, ἠγνοηκέναι κινδυνεύουσι μὲν ὀλίγον ξύμπαντες οἷόν τε ὂν τυγχάνει καὶ δύναμιν ἣν ἔχει, τῶν τε ἄλλων αὐτῆς πέρι καὶ δὴ καὶ γενέσεως, ὡς ἐν πρώτοις ἐστὶ σωμάτων ἔμπροσθεν πάντων γενομένη, καὶ μεταβολῆς τε αὐτῶν καὶ μετακοσμήσεως ἁπάσης ἄρχει παντὸς μᾶλλον p. 892 A ; ἄστρων δὲ δὴ πέρι πάντων καὶ σελήνης ἐνιαυτῶν τε καὶ μηνῶν καὶ πασῶν ὡρῶν πέρι, τίνα ἄλλον λόγον ἐροῦμεν ἢ τὸν αὐτὸν τοῦτον, ὡς ἐπειδὴ ψυχὴ μὲν ἢ ψυχαὶ πάντων τούτων αἴτιαι ἐφάνησαν, ἀγαθαὶ δὲ πᾶσαν ἀρετήν, θεοὺς αὐτὰς εἶναι φήσομεν, εἴτε ἐν σώμασιν ἐνοῦσαι, ζῶα ὄντα, κοσμοῦσι πάντα οὐρανόν, εἴτε ὅπῃ τε καὶ ὅπως; ἔσθ' ὅστις ταῦτα ὁμολογῶν ὑπομενεῖ μὴ θεῶν εἶναι πλήρη πάντα ; p. 899, etc.)

In the *Laws* (probably Plato's latest work) the Ideal theory does not appear. The tenth book is, however, important for the information it gives us on Plato's latest views on cosmology and theology.

INDEX

THE END